Praise for *Made in China*

A *Library Journal* Title to Watch

"The immigrant child longs to be understood and unload her truths, while simultaneously being tasked with preserving her parents' humanity . . . Qu . . . honor[s] these complexities."
—CHANEL MILLER, *The New York Times Book Review*

"Qu's debut memoir untangles the knots of her complicated, traumatic past as she learns the truth about her own history and reckons with the hopes and constraints of the immigrant experience."
—*Time*

"This candid, heartbreaking story centers on an uncommon immigrant narrative featuring a complicated mother-daughter relationship intermingled with the dark side of the pursuit of opportunity in America."
—*Oprah Daily*

"Qu's indelible account of her lonesome childhood should gain her everything she lacked then—confidants, witnesses and fans—who will cheer when she finally reconnects with a long-lost beloved."
—JENNY SHANK, *Star Tribune*

"An important story told with intelligence and heart, a study of discipline as a form of devotion—devotion to a mother, to a legacy, to our own dreams and to those of others, to being good.

So much of American rhetoric is about what we are owed. This graceful memoir is about the much trickier problem of what we deserve. Which is, in the end, brightest love."

—LACY CRAWFORD, author of *Notes on a Silencing*

"Anna Qu masterfully evokes her childhood with a power and grace that speak of an experience that no one should ever have to endure. This moving and unforgettable memoir needs to be read by everyone." —NICOLE DENNIS-BENN, author of *Patsy*

"Anna Qu has written a thoroughly engrossing and nuanced memoir about triumph over trauma and the meaning of home. *Made in China* brings the immigrant experience to life and makes you root for Qu. A must-read." —SOPAN DEB, author of
Missed Translations

"*Made in China* is a sympathetic, brave portrayal of the confusions, difficulties, and hurts that come with growing up between worlds. Anna Qu's writing about her journey as an immigrant deftly shows how our origins—of economic status, of country—have lasting effects on the ways we approach family, work, and self. I was captivated and moved by her story." —ALEXANDRA CHANG,
author of *Days of Distraction*

Made in China

A Memoir of Love and Labor

Anna Qu

Catapult  New York

This book is a memoir. It reflects the author's recollections of experiences over time. Some names and identifying details have been changed to protect the privacy of individuals.

A different version of chapter 11 was published in the fall 2014 issue of *The Threepenny Review* as "Coming Back."

Hardcover ISBN: 978-1-64622-034-2
Paperback ISBN: 978-1-64622-152-3

Cover design by Dana Li
Book design by Jordan Koluch

Library of Congress Control Number: 2020949980

Printed in the United States of America
3 5 7 9 10 8 6 4 2

For Nie Nie,
who taught me to love

I used to think truth was eternal, that once I knew, once I saw, it would be with me forever, a constant by which everything else could be measured. I know now that this isn't so, that most truths are inherently unretainable, that we have to work hard all our lives to remember the most basic things.

—LUCY GREALY

Factory Life

1

The 7 train flooded with natural light as we emerged from underground and Long Island City's graffitied rooftops, prewar buildings, and brick warehouses come into view. The commute from school to my parents' garment factory in Queens was a twenty-five-minute bus ride, a transfer, and then another thirty-five minutes on the subway. After stepping off the packed train, I walked down a sidewalk lined with abandoned warehouses, their windows cloudy, cracked, and boarded up with pieces of plywood. Unmarked trucks and vans passed once in a while. Three long blocks from the station, a large commercial dumpster sat in front of a pair of dark-green double doors. No one went in or out, and there was no way to see inside, but I knew the place. I worked here every day after school and on the weekends. It was my latest punishment.

I used my body as leverage to pull on the metal door. Immediately—even before I was fully in—a gust of stale air lifted the hair off my shoulders and neck, and whipped it around my face. Goose bumps ran along my arms and the back of my neck. The door slammed shut behind me with a mechanical thud, the calm outside disappeared, and the sounds of a working factory took over.

A few tall windows brought in natural light while the rest of the warehouse lay in shadow. The sewing machine section, the only area with any direct lighting, was busy with women wearing disposable masks over their mouths, and forearm coverings. The masks protected against the debris and pollutants in the air, and the oversleeves protected their arms from the heat of the lamps.

From where I stood, I could see two rows of sewing tables, each slightly larger than a school desk, illuminated by individual lamps. Lighting was key to speed and safety here. As the women leaned on the pedals at their feet, their bodies lurched forward in a soft concave, meeting the rhythm of rapid stitches at their fingers. Two shades of maroon thread turned at their spool pins. Once in a while, a hand shot out, tugged on a thread, and unspooled a spindle. I rarely saw faces, only the tops of their backs, circular spotlights exposing the whiteness of their necks.

The only memory I had of the factory before becoming a worker was on Chinese New Year, the one day of the year my parents closed shop. My mother, my half siblings, Henry and Jill, and I came early in the mornings to stuff gift bags. We formed an assembly line; I was at the head, a reluctant Henry stood next to me, followed by Jill, and then my mother. She sat licking the tip of her index finger, peeling crisp twenties and sealing them in red envelopes. It was hard to keep Henry working for more than a few minutes at a time, but Jill, a year younger than him, loved chores and tasks. She tossed a handful of red candy into each plastic bag, one eye always on our mother, seeking assurance and approval.

I remembered the warehouse feeling cavernous, cold, and quiet. Our voices carried over the entire space. The vast size made us giddy, nervous. I remembered running from the echoes that lurked in the shadows like waiting ghosts. We raced back to our mother, and back to complete our task. A running factory filled with workers was worlds apart from the deserted warehouse where we played Chinese Santa Claus. But from the number of gift bags we put together, I knew there were about fifty regular employees. There was no way to count the people in the factory now, tucked behind and around the machines, moving from one station to another. The enormity of the warehouse intimidated me still.

A long thread landed in the corner of my mouth and I wiped my face with the back of my sleeve. Industrial metal fans strategically placed around the warehouse circulated flat, hot air. The constant turbulence was meant to provide relief, but instead it annoyed and unsettled. Trash, loose thread, plastic, lint, and pieces of fabric migrated from the nearby surfaces, crevices, and floors, revolving in the air until they caught on something or someone. I looked over to the office, where my mother was most likely doing inventory, planning new projects, or handling payroll. Then I headed in the opposite direction. I passed an old, dank fridge next to a small island with an off-white microwave and a commercial-sized rice cooker that could feed all the workers. Past the kitchen was the women's restroom. A light bulb flickered on and off, and then on again. The smell of ammonia mingled with rice and leftovers hit me as I passed by.

To my left, I paused as an older Chinese man shouted urgently to a younger man, his voice drowned out by the hiss of the steam press they operated. It was a father and son. Or an uncle and nephew. I wasn't sure which, but they were close enough to my station that I was familiar with their routine. They operated a commercial steamer with an extended hose on a tall rack for garments. Steam rose out of a wide head or out of the large iron resting on the oversized board. Their station was one of the reasons the factory was always hotter and more humid than it was outside. The father manned the machine, the more dangerous job, while the son ran inventory, pulling clothing off the steamer hook or iron press, and then quickly folding and packaging them in boxes or clear garment bags on racks. Their speed and intimacy made it look easy, but they were both drenched in sweat.

Up close, they were older than I thought. The older man could have been in his fifties. He lifted a lever and quickly moved out of the way. Steam rose in a white cloud above them and was swiftly picked up by the fans, leaving a metallic humidity in the air. The smell reminded me of the first day we turned the heat on in the winter. The son swooped in and lifted the shirt off the press. Each piece was newly starched and pressed before they left the factory. He worked hastily, turning to lift the next shirt off.

A short, weathered Chinese man hurried by, dumping black trash bags of fabric and thread a few feet from where I stood. It was Mr. Wang, my mother's eyes and ears. I pulled another loose thread from my lip and picked up my pace.

Hip-hop music was coming from my station as I approached. Six women stood around a long wood table, each holding a bundle of fabric in their hands. The cutting girls, as I liked to call them, shifted and made room for me. I dropped my Jansport book bag on the concrete floor and felt something wrap around my ankle. We stood close to two fans, and they often blew fabric, thread, and pieces of paper off the table and onto us. Without glancing down, I used my free leg to kick whatever it was off.

One of the younger women, the jester in the group, was swaying from side to side and humming. She always drew smiles and laughter from the other women. Once in a while, she'd hear a song that got her dancing. Her energy was so contagious, she could get the whole team moving to the same rhythm. I gave her a quick smile as I pulled my hair from my face and up in a ponytail, in preparation for my work.

My job was to cut loose thread off half-completed or finished articles of clothing. An unfamiliar mountain of maroon fabric sat at the center of the table. We must have received a new order this morning. I motioned at an older woman at the end of the table with my free hand. If new inventory came in and I was at school, she showed me what to do. She seemed to be the natural leader of the table. She often quieted us if we grew too playful and garnered looks from other workers. She moved slowly, but somehow managed to accomplish tasks nimbly and efficiently.

"Tranquillo," she said during the first weekend I worked. She put her hand over my scissors and gave them a shake. I was working too fast, giving myself another blister. I wanted the long work-day to be over, but she understood something I didn't—moving faster didn't make the day go faster. If we finished this project, there would be another. There would always be another project.

"Tran-quillo," she said one final time.

Our group worked on orders as a collective. Some orders took a couple of days while others took weeks or a month to complete. We never knew how many more days, how many bundles of fabric were left, or if there was a deadline. There was a large bin near the table, and as long as that bin was filled, we had work to do. It was our job to keep our heads down, do the work, and not ask questions. The rules at the factory weren't so different from the rules at home.

My thread trimmers were exactly where I'd left them. I was the latest member to join the table, so I was left with a pair of scissors no one wanted. They were dull except at the very tip. To use them effectively, I had to snip as hard as I could at just the right angle. Otherwise, the dull blade would require three to four snips. As soon as I picked them up, the inner ring rubbed an open blister between my thumb and index finger. It was impossible to keep the wound clean.

The older woman caught my wave and nodded. The girl next to me shifted to let her in. Like most low-skilled workers here, we were paid by the hour. We stood in the same spot day in and day out. Our projects varied from cutting loose threads to tying knots and bows, to gluing patterns. It was menial, tedious, relentless work. We stood in place, shifting our weight from one foot to the other. Our feet and ankles swelling, necks and shoulders cramping, backs aching. We developed sores, blisters, calluses from the repetitive motions as we trimmed, cut, knotted, and on occasion glued, tied, and folded. We developed lean shoulders, thick calves. The tasks generally took a few seconds to learn but were endless in execution. The only time we looked up or moved was to collect more work. Everyone watched the clock; how quickly we worked was the only bit of control we had. If we could enjoy a song on the radio, it was time we gained back. For three to five minutes, our minds could be elsewhere. We saw it as a form of freedom.

Like any other job, there was a hierarchy at the factory. There was management: my parents, Mr. Wang, and an accountant, who did everything from procuring deals, to mocking up prototypes as samples, to paying the workers. There were the fabric cutters who cut shapes out of yards of raw fabric, the sewers at the sewing station who put the raw pieces together, the women at our table who trimmed, the runners who moved inventory in and around the factory, the steamers and packers who readied the final products, and the drivers who picked up supplies and dropped off orders. The Chinese workers, who spoke the same language as the management, had access to more information, competitive pay, and, sometimes, the freedom to come and go. One of the unspoken policies was that the more skilled the worker, the fewer limitations there were. For example, the quick-fingered sewers were paid per item instead of per hour. Most pieces paid between half a cent and five cents each, and the amount of money each sewer made depended on their speed and the amount of time they wanted to put in. They all competed on the orders that were quickest to finish and paid the most, and sometimes that meant forgoing lunch and bathroom breaks, and working overtime and on Sundays. When lucrative projects came in, they worked non-stop, but they also had the freedom to take days off when things were slow. Rumor had it, some of the skilled sewers worked at other sweatshops like independent contractors. There were at least three seats vacant today.

Up close, the older woman was shorter, her body rounder. Her hair was pulled back in a tight, gelled ponytail, like the rest of the women. She had a shiny coat of lip gloss on, but wore no other makeup. In her hand, she brought the shirt she was working on. I nodded as she spoke in Spanish. Whenever I thought I knew what she was saying, the meaning disappeared. Fortunately, our tasks were never complicated, and I could follow her just by watching her hands. It was no different than when I first started elementary school and spent the first few years deciphering what I needed from body language, facial expressions, gestures, and pauses.

She turned the Henley shirt until it was facing us and began to cut the loose strings from the sleeves. Then, with expert maneuvering, she used the tips of her clippers to tease the strands of loose thread out from under and around the three buttons along the collar. She made two snips and excess thread fell onto the table. Immediately, the fan picked up the thread and it skated off. I could see that the sewers had used one continuous thread to sew all three buttons for speed, and it was our job to clean up their work. I nodded again, said gracias, and grabbed a stack of shirts to work on.

Each snip dug into the old broken blister on my hand. I clenched my teeth and focused on teasing the maroon thread around the black buttons. The tips of my clippers felt clumsy compared with the demonstration I'd just seen. My hand throbbed and felt hot to the touch. But methodically, I clipped the loose thread from each sleeve and then around the buttons one at a time. After a dozen shirts, I settled in.

—

I've never been very good at waiting. As a toddler, after my mother left me with Nie Nie and Azi, my grandparents, to follow the path to the American dream, I learned to wait for her return. I waited through breaths, meals, baths, fights with my Azi, rides on my bike; I waited until wounds from my scrapes scabbed and healed, until my hair grew long enough for two tight braids, until holes spread in my underwear. As a child, every year stretched longer than the life I had lived, and soon, I could no longer remember what it felt like to have a mother, only what it was like to be without one.

"Ka la, ka la," they said, *soon soon*. They were the soothers—my grandmother, aunts, cousins, and even my mother over the static landline. Neighbors and Nie Nie's friends joined in, balancing their tongues on the roofs of their mouths to make the same sounds until they played on a loop in my head. *Ka la, ka la*. When the neighborhood boys taunted me because I was fatherless and now motherless, I repeated the words in my mind like a mantra. *Ka la, ka la*.

No one knew how long it would take for her to return, not even my mother. Time passed as it does, pity turned into stretches of silence, and silence turned into awkwardness and avoidance.

I was the girl without parents; a father dead, a mother who left Wenzhou, China, to start a new life. The waiting for my mother's failing promise steeped like tea, growing dark and bitter, coloring everything and finding its way into my interactions with others. I took it out on my grandparents, on girls trying to be my friends, on boys who refused to be my friends. I was wild, angry, and resentful of the community that took pity on me because *ka la* had turned into five years and the cadences in their hushed voices now told me my mother would never come.

———

In 1991, when I was seven years old, my mother finally reappeared in my life. Azi, Nie Nie, and I bathed with water heated from the stove. We carefully combed and parted our hair, dressed in our best outfits, and set out before the neighborhood rooster's first crow. We spent half the morning traveling to the city by boat and then by bus. It was the first time I saw my grandparents disoriented, their eyes darting around the congested streets, loud vendors shouting, and hordes of city people moving impatiently with places to go. They looked frail in their oversized clothes, eager expressions, and tight handgrips.

The heels of my mother's three-inch stilettos, echoing down the long corridor of Wenzhou International Airport, announced her arrival. Somehow after an eighteen-hour flight, she was wearing pressed business slacks and a perfectly starched white shirt. Her hair was fashionably cropped, dyed, and styled, and her face was freshly made up. When she stopped in front of us, and the waiting finally came to an end, I didn't recognize her. I hid behind Nie Nie's slacks, shielding myself from the confrontation, from the person for whom I'd waited five long years. Nie Nie yanked me from behind her, told me to greet my mother. "Call her Mother," she said. I recognized the stranger's voice from the staticky phone calls we had every two weeks, but I held tightly to Nie Nie's leg, too overwhelmed by the newness of having a mother to respond.

She had been away long enough to learn to dress well and leave behind her country manners. Azi called it "acting big." His daughter had made it, and like China's disillusioned leader, she had made sacrifices for a greater good, and was now transformed. It wasn't customary for adults to be physical, so my mother only exchanged words with her father and reached for her mother's arm affectionately.

After she spoke to both of them for a few minutes, she squatted down on her heels. Her face, inches from mine, rang a command. *You know me, I'm your mother. You know me.*

———

I saw brick inside a house for the first time when I reached my new home in Queens. In Wenzhou, houses were gray and made of cement. This house had red brick on the inside and outside, and I could make out each individual brick if I stood close enough. The fireplace was evenly laid with shades of burnt orange, crimson, and maroon bricks, individually separated by an inch of coarse taupe mortar. They were seated in a perfect line. I wanted to run my fingertips along and count them. The wall was the first thing I noticed after walking into the fluorescent interior of my new home, right before I was introduced to Henry and Jill.

I must have been a forgetful child, because I don't recall the initial shock at meeting my mother's other children. My parents were still new to me—I had just met my stepfather at the airport, and I was still unsure if I recognized my mother. She had the familiarity of someone I once knew, but no longer felt close to. That had not changed. Within the first week, I was made aware of and sensitive to the differences between the way she treated my half siblings and me.

Henry received the first and last serving at every meal after my stepfather. Jill had almost as many clothes as my mother, outfits of matching shoes, hair bands, and coats. My mother was generous with clothing, food, treats, and toys, but only with them. It was soon clear that I shouldn't expect to be treated the same way. I was not supposed to ask for the Yan Yan chocolate-dipped sticks, almond cookies, fruit chews, and egg tarts that were brought home. They were not meant for me, the girl with no father. Nice things were meant for the children whose father was providing for us all, and I should not compare myself with them. I quickly learned that it was petty to point out these obvious differences and rude to make assumptions about my share. In order to live in "their" house, as my mother harshly whispered in Wenzhounese, it was best not to mention the small moments of discrimination, even as they grew, in my view, insurmountable.

Almost immediately, I felt the segregation created by language. My mother had plucked me from Wenzhou, but Wenzhou had come with me. I was the only person to whom my mother spoke Wenzhounese, the only member of the household with the same past. Manners, pleasantries, and kindnesses were in Mandarin. Teaching me to be ladylike, to cater to my half siblings and my stepfather, was done in our secret native tongue, now the disciplinary tone. Things she didn't want the other children to know, things she couldn't say in Mandarin, she said in Wenzhounese. Mandarin, the dialect she shared with her new husband and their kids, allowed her to leave her past, her poor roots behind. Mandarin would be a class improvement she would teach me.

In the years that followed, my sense of betrayal divided me from almost every single person. I blamed the situation on those I felt most comfortable with—my grandparents, who failed to inform me of my new situation, who were now seven thousand miles away and could no longer protect me. They had let my mother take me. On the phone, I ached to tell Nie Nie how much I hated it here. I wanted to go back home to our place above the hardware store, back to the unpaved dirt roads where I ran barefoot with other kids, back to a place where I could be an only child again. But I knew instinctively not to verbalize the deepening resentment, the inequality I saw. The desire to go back was preposterous and disrespectful considering how much everyone had sacrificed and how long I had waited. The yearning sat in my throat instead, collecting into unspoken shame. I stood mute during those expensive and short calls, twirling the phone cord around my index finger and then around my whole hand until it reached my wrist. I let Nie Nie finish her irrelevant questions—*Have you eaten lunch yet? Are you warm enough? Do you listen to your mother?*—and waited for the call to end.

My parents went back to work at the garment factory immediately after we arrived in New York, and I enrolled in a public school that, noting my lack of exposure to English, put me in first rather than second grade.

My classmates had homemade snacks in Ziploc bags, lunches with sides and desserts, and favorite toys tucked in pockets of their book bags. They had more than one pair of shoes they rotated daily. I was envious of the books that weren't required for class, games I never knew existed, and toys beyond my wildest imagination. Where did they come from? Who told them about these toys? During show-and-tell, they brought new toys and stories of weekend trips with their family. I sensed the freedom they enjoyed and felt an incomprehensible loss.

One day, I was sent home from school with a note that had words like *sanitary* and *cleanliness*. Even though I wasn't playing outside regularly, it made the students and the teacher uncomfortable that I came to class on consecutive days in the same outfit. In China, we didn't bathe daily, no one did. Bathhouses were once-a-week trips. Like my grandmother, my mother kept a meticulous home, and the notice was such an insult to her pride that she dragged me into the bathroom right then and there. She scrubbed me pink, hissed that I needed to bathe every weekday from then on. The next day, she brought extra clothes from the factory in a plastic bag. They still smelled processed and pressed, and they made my skin itch. Since the factory only made adult clothing, my mother had sewed them herself with smaller measurements. Still, they fit baggy and long, and felt coarse and ugly. It would take almost a full year in school for me to understand my new clothes made me stand out just as much as before. All the kids wore jeans, shirts with buttons and collars, dresses with lace and pleats. They were detailed clothes bought from department stores or boutiques, not haphazardly sewn in a sweatshop. Once comprehended, the shame was inescapable. I thought about how in China, no one had much more than I did, but here in Queens, I didn't even understand the frameworks within which people lived, the limits of what they owned. It was more than toys and books. Here the teachers were not allowed to reprimand you, for example, and if they hit you, parents complained. Where I came from, hitting was approved. It meant someone was minding your child. In my hometown, children ran wild without bathing, without curfews, and the kids I chased around the neighborhood barefoot were just like me. Everything felt backward, too orderly, and full of rules.

As my parents' first child to go to school, I was battling ignorance from both directions. If I said I didn't know how to do my homework, the teacher's response would always be the same: Ask an adult at home. Ask your parents. My parents didn't understand why children were treated as such precious beings and had no idea why there were so many parent-teacher conferences, opportunities to come along on class trips, bring treats to share with the class, and participate with other parents in neighborhood groups. *Don't they work?* my mother demanded. And the teachers seemed unable to understand that my parents put in ten-to-fourteen-hour days and couldn't get out of work to meet with them. It became clear that teachers favored students with active parents, parents they could talk to and work with. I saw it every year, in every new class, each teacher would pay just a little bit more attention to the kids whose parents had come to conferences, had dropped off cupcakes, had picked their kids up after school.

To their credit, my parents did realize I needed help they could not provide. They saw the language gap and the trouble I was having and started looking around for a tutor. They didn't know the first thing about it, so they approached the school. My first tutor, if I remember correctly, was the old nurse at my elementary school. She was hard of hearing, moved excruciatingly slowly, and wasn't much help with second-grade homework, but at the very least, I was able to practice English.

———

By the decorative fireplace, I witnessed my parents' first house party. It was a couple of months after I arrived in New York and, in fact, it was in my honor. After my mother came to the United States, she worked hard, caught the eye of the owner of the sweatshop she worked in, remarried, and had two kids. Not only had she succeeded in making her American dream come true, she had also managed to bring her seven-year-old daughter with her. It was an achievement worth celebrating. Each milestone had so far been hidden for fear of envy and interference until this very moment, when it was finally achieved.

Everyone from my mother's side of the family gathered in our house. Aunts and uncles I hadn't seen for years, hadn't known were in the United States, showed up. My aunts crowded me, whispered how much I looked like my father. *An exact replica*, one whispered. *You're right!* an aunt-in-law confirmed, but then quickly changed the subject when they saw my mother's grim expression. She didn't like to talk about the past, and especially not about him.

They asked if I remembered my cousins. My aunts' and uncles' kids were still in China. *You have to remember them, they took such good care of you.* They looked pained, their regrets a dewiness in their eyes, when I shied away, unable to say. *Lo Ta? A Mue, Yoke.* They missed their children, but it was better to build a future for your kids than to stay by their side. And this party, celebrating the union of mother and daughter, was proof that their children would also be by their side one day. It was possible.

My mother gave a guided tour of our duplex house. My aunts complimented the feng shui of the windows and doors, and the spacious, immaculate kitchen. Upstairs they exclaimed in hushed voices about the size of the bedrooms, the number of bathrooms, and the unobstructed view of the street and front yard. My uncles were most impressed by the front lawn—grass in Wenzhou was rare and only landscaped around monuments and government buildings, not personal property. The tour acknowledged the first home purchased in America. My mother, youngest of her five siblings, was the first to own property. She paused at the right places, collected the approvals, and when it was all over, gathered everyone back in the living room.

I was supposed to remember my relatives, but they felt like blurs of a family I once knew. Four aunts and four uncles, and I couldn't figure out who was married to whom and who their kids were. I sat down on the freshly waxed leather couch, bored of watching the adults ignore me.

"Let the guests sit first," my mother hissed for the second time since I had gotten dressed.

She was teaching me guaichu, which in Mandarin meant manners. In Wenzhou, my grandparents let me spend the day playing with the neighborhood kids until it grew dark and I grew hungry. In America, where I was learning Mandarin and English, my bad behavior and wild ways would not be tolerated. I was to come straight home from school and never play outside. Girls did not fight with boys, girls did not get dirty, girls did not run and fall, girls did not get angry. Children were to move when told, speak only when spoken to, and always, always be obedient. It was her job to break my bad habits and make sure I didn't act like the rabid dog my grandparents raised.

She followed me with her eyes as I got up. Her narrowing gaze, I learned, missed nothing. I tucked my bare toes under the couch and leaned against the wall. Her lips pulled into a thin, taut line before her eyes reluctantly turned back to the party.

My stepfather, or Baba as I was told to call him, was fiddling with the knobs on the black box that sat behind the glass door of the entertainment center. He flipped through the channels until the TV lit up a vibrant blue. In a few seconds, music blasted from the speakers and the TV flashed to a couple holding hands, walking down a path. Brown leaves and pink cherry blossom petals cascaded around them like wedding confetti. Words appeared on the bottom of the screen, slowly changing color.

"Who wants to sing first?" my mother said in a cheery voice.

I was always surprised by the quick change in her moods. It felt like she was always only angry with me, and when she turned her attention to my half siblings or my stepfather her anger disappeared. She held the slender microphone out to my uncles and smiled. Her bright auburn hair was blown out and hair-sprayed to a compliant bob. Her navy dress clung like the skin of a fruit, conservative around the collar, just above the knee. A pair of powder-pink slippers covered her feet.

"You sing," my oldest uncle, the one with long, bony legs and goofy glasses said. My uncles were so thin their hip bones were visible through their loose jeans, cinched at the waist by wide belts. Tall, thin laborers accustomed to long hours in poor conditions too common to workers like him.

"No," my mother said in a don't-be-silly tone, waving him off. "Sing a duet with your husband!"

No one reached for the mic, so she gently rested it on the coffee table. She picked up a pair of empty glasses between two fingers and slipped into the kitchen, leaving her siblings to decide among themselves. By the second song, my uncles were sharing the mic and my aunts were loudly singing the chorus and swaying to the lyrics.

At the height of the party, my mother sat down next to my stepfather and relaxed. Neither had had a chance to sit since the doorbell started ringing with guests. His face was beginning to darken to a red hue around the temples and cheekbones as the evening progressed and he drank more.

"Okay, come on, it's your turn," my older aunt said, bringing the attention back to them.

"We've all sung," my second aunt nudged.

"Here, take it," my second uncle said to my stepfather, his Mandarin beginning to slur from alcohol. My stepfather accepted the microphone and then the disk cover. A light flutey song started and a new Chinese couple appeared on the screen. My aunts clapped and my uncles gave loud approving whistles. An old classic duet.

My stepfather's voice came in smooth like the oval glass of cognac in his spare hand. He caught the beat and carried it in the right places. My mother seemed shy, girly, and uncharacteristically insecure. Her cheeks flushed and her forehead dampened in embarrassment. Her voice was sharp and off pitch, like she was raising her speaking voice. He sang her parts until they were singing both the male and female lyrics together, despite what the pink and baby-blue lines on the screen dictated. His head, with sideswept hair, leaned into her bob as the song came to an end. I'd never seen them intimate before. It was rare to see my mother relaxed or enjoying herself. My aunts clapped, and she laughed.

The women decided to clear out of the living room after the duet, leaving the men to smoke, drink, and talk about things men talked about. They gathered in the warmly lit kitchen and sat around the glass table with cups of flowering oolong tea. On a lazy Susan, my mother had put out an array of snacks: loose pistachios, dried pineapple candy, and roasted sunflower seeds surrounded by plates of freshly sliced cantaloupe, square-cut watermelon, and pears in naked quarters. We didn't know much about how to throw parties, so the snacks mirrored items put out during Chinese New Year's Eve celebrations.

I wandered back and forth between the living room of men

and the kitchen of women, feeling restless and out of place. There were no other children; my one-year-old half sister and two-year-old half brother had been put to bed hours ago.

My stepfather was sitting in his leather armchair, the one he often snored off in before bed. My uncles had fallen back into speaking Wenzhounese with one another, forgetting that he didn't understand the dialect. My stepfather didn't interrupt or intercept their conversations, though, remaining courteous and aloof.

Sipping his cognac, he caught my reflection in the TV.

"A-Na," he said in Mandarin. "Guo lai."

He reached over and placed his drink on the corner of the coffee table. He motioned with his hand and I walked over.

"Do you like it here?" he asked in Mandarin, leaning in over his growing belly and pressed gray slacks.

My mother had warned me not to bother my stepfather. He worked all day and he needed rest. I was to be quiet and obedient around him; he was the reason I was able to come to America and live in such a nice house. I felt shy all of a sudden. I had never had a father before, or not one I remembered. What did one say to a father? What did one say to a father who was not really your father? I looked down at my right hand resting on the soft brown leather. It was warm; his hand must have been on the same spot. We hadn't spoken much, and we were rarely alone together, but I always liked the sound of his voice and the way his smile reached his eyes.

"Do you understand me?" he asked when I didn't respond.

I was learning to communicate with him and my half siblings

in Mandarin. Another change in a sea of changes washing over me. Mandarin was not as difficult as learning English, but understanding the dynamic at home felt more wary and daunting than assimilating to the foreignness of school.

I nodded. It was true that I was to call him Baba, but I didn't have the same right to him that my half siblings had. I thought maybe if I was really, *really* good, and did everything perfectly, I could earn some of the affection he had for Henry and Jill.

"Are you happy here? Do you like it here?" he asked, his flushed face so close, I inhaled a wave of Rémy XO. His deep-set eyes were bloodshot and smaller than usual.

I nodded, and added, "Uh-huh."

He put a hand on each side of my shoulders and pulled me to his body for an embrace. A heavy scent of alcohol and cigarettes enveloped me. I remained still, his breathing moving our bodies, and then I wrestled out of the warmth. The only physical contact I had was with my mother when she dragged me across Main Street in Flushing, bruising my forearm all the way to Jin San, our local Chinese supermarket. We were many things, but affectionate was not one of them. Males and females were usually separated and contact was considered inappropriate unless they were related by blood. And even then, touching was rare between fathers and daughters. Decorum must be maintained. I remembered my mother stressing that my stepfather was a man and there were things that were improper.

Needing to be near the women, I gravitated to the circle around the kitchen table. My mother turned and I realized I had put my hand on her thin arm.

"Hah?" she asked. Her almond eyes narrowed to a sliver, just the way they did whenever she thought I was lying. "Ju nie a?" *What?*

"Gi . . ." I start in Wenzhounese, searching for the unfamiliar word. I wrapped my arms around myself, unable to remember the uncommonly used word for hug, and switched to Mandarin. "Bao wuo."

Who did? She put her arm on my shoulder and shook. *Who?*

"Baba."

She blinked and looked at me as if there was something smeared on my face. I felt weird. Why was I telling her this? It was a good thing, wasn't it? A hug meant he liked me and maybe he could have the same relationship with me, as with his daughter.

She stood up. The legs of the wooden chair scraped harshly against the tiled floor. My aunts looked up, pausing their conversation about how to make fish dumpling soup—the ingredients could be found, but the flavor was still not right. Everything tasted different here.

My mother stormed through the door to the living room, head held high. When I got to the other side of the door, my parents were standing and facing each other. The TV screen behind them, showing a turning disco ball, silhouetted their faces in profile. My mother was shouting with her hand inches from his surprised face. She pointed at me without looking in my direction, and I shrank back involuntarily. I had never seen her so angry with anyone besides me.

"I didn't!" he finally forced out.

Someone turned the lights on. We blinked against the overhead light and the abrupt stillness. My aunts, emerging from the kitchen, surveyed the situation.

"What is going on?" my second aunt asked. She looked at the men for answers. They shrugged and then looked in my direction.

"Come on," she continued, "this is a happy occasion. Don't ruin it."

"You know children," my oldest aunt said, touching my mother's forearm. She jerked away from my aunt's touch.

"He's drunk. And he touched her!" my mother shouted.

"What are you talking about? I'm sure that didn't happen." My aunt's voice held an older sibling's warning.

My stepfather's face drained of his drunken flush as he registered the accusation and sobered up.

All the eyes in the room were on them and then on me. My aunts stood at my mother's elbows. My older aunt cleared her throat and warned, "Don't say it like that, that sounds ugly."

"Children don't know what they're talking about sometimes. You know that," my second aunt purred. "Right, Na? Everything is fine, nothing happened."

She frowned at me, a look of regret on her face.

I took another step back and felt the fireplace behind me. The grainy brick felt cool and coarse against my perspiring hands. My cheeks burned and I looked down. Everyone was wearing the new house slippers my mother had bought for the party. I looked from my mother's accusing eyes to my stepfather's glossy ones and thought back to when their heads were pressed together, their faces illuminated in a bluish hue. I sensed I had caused a rift between my parents, one that I would pay for later. One thing was clear: this was my fault. The tension in the room and all of my aunts' and uncles' eyes confirmed that I had ruined the night.

I nodded, rubbing my hand on crimson brick over and over.

"See? She knows she's wrong. Everything is fine now."

"Come on." My aunts led my mother up the stairs like a pair of bodyguards.

"Kids these days," one of my uncles mumbled after they were gone.

The party was over and reality had found us. My uncles stood, sobering under the bright recessed lighting. My aunts cleared the last of the glasses and carried them to the sink. My oldest aunt whispered it was time to go, and then they let themselves out.

———

My mother set new rules for how things would be after the drunken embrace. After that night, she was impatient, calculating, hasty to reprimand and overcorrect. I had to be separated from the other children, I had to be separated from my stepfather, I had to be taught better.

Pull the hair back from your face. Don't slouch. Don't lean. Straighten up. Don't just sit there. Why are you standing? What have you been doing while I've been working all day?

When I started elementary school, my stepfather taught me the alphabet. Before dinner, he would wrap his large tanned hand tightly around mine and show me how to trace the letters. I would sit at the kitchen table and swing my heel against the legs of the chair, copying the letters in my black-and-white composition notebook. We got stuck on *S*, so he'd teach me to curve my *S* the right way. On the following night, after I traced the two pages he'd assigned, I'd show him my progress. The letter had turned into a mirror image along the way and he'd teach me to correct it.

After the party, he no longer traced my letters. He scanned the page, nodded briskly, and said "Okay" before turning back to his Taiwanese paper. We never finished the alphabet. He began ignoring and avoiding me. When I had a permission slip sent home, he said it had to go to my mother. I told him she couldn't read English, only he could. He shrugged, and repeated himself. The thin permission slip felt suddenly heavy in my hand as I went to find my mother. She was in the master bedroom, and when I stood next to her, I was silent. She didn't look up from her nightly skin regimen, but told me to leave it on her vanity table.

In the morning, she reappeared with the sheet of paper signed in my stepfather's slanted handwriting. That was how our relationship solidified, my mother guarding us both, standing between my stepfather and me.

2

Every weekend, when I worked full days at the factory, the most exciting thing happened at noon. Lint, threads, and loose paper fell to the ground and all the sound came to a halt. My coworkers moved toward the wall, where a long line was already forming. Only the sewers, who were paid on commission, were exempt from clocking in and out at lunchtime.

In the kitchen, a white cloud of steam rose to the height of the ceiling, filling the area with the aroma of rice. The rice was provided by the factory, a perk for all workers, but only the Chinese workers seemed to bring leftovers daily. At first, I thought I'd eat lunch with my parents when I worked on weekends, but they packed leftovers like they always did. "There isn't enough food for you," my mother said, separating me from them. She gave me five dollars and told me to buy lunch. I wasn't surprised, but I kicked myself for hoping otherwise, for asking.

When lunchtime came around on my first weekend, I went to the kitchen to look for a Chinese person. There was a thin, tired-looking woman heating up her lunch. She shouted that she didn't know where to buy food and waved me off, an exhausted look on her face. Embarrassed, I turned back to my station. Only two women were hanging around, the rest had taken off.

"Donde . . . comida?" I asked, losing the sentence I'd practiced all morning in my head. I made a plate with my left hand and motioned eating with my right.

Most of the Spanish-speaking workers got lunch from the same spots, but now they seemed to be debating where to direct me. They were mostly women from Mexico, and even though I was taking Spanish as my secondary language at school, they spoke too fast for me to follow. After a few minutes of pointing, I was able to figure out that I should turn left after two blocks. The place they directed me to was a converted Chinese takeout restaurant serving Mexican food. When I got there, I could see a Chinese man working in the kitchen, running to keep up with the orders. I ordered chicken with rice, and handed over my five dollars.

On the way back, on nice days, I'd see workers sitting on the sidewalk curb outside the building. Otherwise, we sat on stools brought from home or empty chairs. It was gloriously silent in that hour. Sometimes the sewers went back to work before the hour was up, trying to add a few additional pieces to their daily count. The buzz of needles kept us company as we ate our meals out of foam to-go boxes. Promptly at 1:00 p.m., the machines turned back on, and then the unforgiving fans. Within a few minutes it was as if the break had never taken place.

Sometimes after lunch, I kept an eye on the swinging office door, which I could see if I stood toward the end of the table. When my mother appeared, she dropped fabric and samples off or exchanged words with the Chinese workers on the sewing machine. I rarely saw her looking around or walking the floor.

The cutting girls were an optimistic bunch, their lips moving as often as their hands. I liked the way their voices grew familiar, their giggles and soft tones bringing me back to a period in my life when I was surrounded by women, a time before conversations made much sense but when sounds did. Since none of them spoke English, I had plenty of time to myself. It occurred to me then that my greatest loss was the feeling of community, the way these women got along with one another and lifted the whole group with shared stories, advice, and companionship. In Wenzhou, Nie Nie always surrounded herself with neighbors, friends, and family. She traded favors, and used knowledge and news as currency. She wrapped her community around her like a security blanket, always willing to share what she had and always on the lookout for something good for her family and friends. There was a festivity in the way she lived that was lost in the red-brick house where I lived with my mother. Our house was clean and new, and we had everything we needed, but it was cold and quiet and everything had its place.

My mother kept her distance from friends; people that helped her when she first came to New York, women with whom she traded favors, acquaintances that she met working the sewing station. As her position changed, it changed her. She weaned herself away, or enough so that when she was home, no one bothered her. It was a stark difference from the way my grandmother lived, from the warm memories I held of her kitchen, where everyone was encouraged to drop by for conversation and tea. No one was encouraged to come over in my new home.

Money changed relationships, perhaps especially with family. My mother's ambivalence meant she shied away from everyone, but she was still close to her siblings. I learned early on that her older siblings would reprimand her if I complained enough to them about the way she treated me. I tattled on her, hoping to be saved. Of course, my complaining only made things worse. Her anger flared. I was her daughter, and no one could tell her what to do. She didn't care for reasoning or advice, especially from family that often asked for her help. She chose to keep me from their prying eyes and ears. It was easy enough; they rarely came over to our house, and when they called on the phone, my mother made sure she was the one who answered. When they invited our family over for Chinese New Year's Eve, lantern or mid-autumn festivals, and other holidays, she wordlessly left me at home. I looked around at the Chinese workers and wondered if I'd recognize any of my relatives if I saw them. Did they stop by the factory? Was one of my aunts on the sewing machine? Being with the cutting girls every day, I was reminded of my isolation, a loneliness that felt large enough to swallow the world.

—

My identity and situation were unique at the sweatshop. Even though I was working forty to fifty hours a week, I was a part-time employee. I was the bosses' kid. I was getting an education and could speak English. My parents weren't kind or generous, but they owned a house and could afford a maid, tutors, and someone to cut our grass every week. Just by my proximity to my mother, I was fortunate. The combination of those factors meant I did not fit in the sweatshop. I did not rely on the sweatshop for my survival. They sensed, like I did, that my arrangement was temporary.

My parents usually left the factory before I did so that they could have dinner with Henry and Jill as a family. It took them about thirty minutes to drive home if there wasn't too much traffic, but it took me an hour and a half. I couldn't see what time it was from where I stood, but we all knew when it was 8:00 p.m. One by one the machines and then the fans went silent. I could finally hear the women around me move: the sound of the clippers coming to rest on the table, the hoarse exhalations as they stretched from a long day of standing, the sound of shoes against the cement floors as they walked out, the slam of the heavy double doors. In a matter of seconds, our hearing was returned to us.

One evening, I found a seat on the 7 train headed home. I pulled out my social studies textbook, and was reading when a man standing over me bumped into me. I looked up to find an erect penis at eye level. He had unzipped his pants and gotten his dick out without anyone noticing. I looked around for someone who might be seeing what I was seeing. No one made eye contact, no one moved. Soundlessly, I pulled the textbook up to my chest, and then over my chin and nose, as a barrier. I sat back against the seat. As the train lurched and turned, his swollen penis moved at me. I shoved my textbook out like a shield. His face was leathery and he was old, possibly drunk. He avoided my eyes and pretended nothing was out of place. My arms strained; my mind raced. I felt a tap and then a thump against my textbook. Should I get up and run out at the next stop? What if he followed me? It'd be worse to be caught on a platform alone with him. We pulled into the next station and the doors swung open. He walked out, his dick pointing in the direction he was headed. A few heads turned when I burst into tears and we pulled away from the station.

When I arrived home, darkness met me. The house was still. The lights on the first floor were turned off and my half siblings were asleep, but I could hear the TV coming from my parents' room. Shoes off, I moved barefoot through the living room. I touched the leather couch as I passed by, then the plastic-protected dining room set, moving deeper into the house.

Dinner sat wrapped in plastic on the kitchen counter. The rice cooker was still on, and when I lifted the lid, white steam blossomed into the dark. It reminded me of the father-and-son team at the factory, exerting themselves before the steam press, each hoping to relieve the other's load. I opened my mouth and shoved in scoops of hot rice. The gulps of warm, glutinous grain warmed the stiffness in my chest. An understanding hit me as I swallowed the scalding rice—I was alone and vulnerable to whatever that guy had wanted to do on the train. I was lucky nothing worse had happened, but luck, I was learning, didn't make me feel better. Lucky meant being grateful and alone, lucky meant swallowing injustice and unfairness. Lifting another scoop of rice into my mouth, knowing I should have been relieved, I began to cry. Was it because I was an immigrant? A child without the protection of an adult? Or because I was a girl on a train at night?

Removing the shrink-wrap revealed shredded pork and carrots, napa cabbage, ginger-and-scallion-steamed fish, and minced beef with tomatoes. I ate without turning the lights on, learning that if you can't see your food, you taste it less, too. There was no one to talk to about what happened to me on the train, no one to confide in. I was a ghost haunting a family that wanted nothing to do with me, and the loneliness left a void food could not fill.

Years ago, during the summer months, Henry, Jill, and I used to catch fireflies in our backyard. Just after dinner, when the overbearing heat relented, the sun stalled lazily against the low horizon, and the earth cooled to the touch, we'd run barefoot over the freshly cut grass that our neighbor Bob mowed for us. The still warm grass under our feet made us daring; we leaped, pranced, and hooted. We were wild children, and the nostalgia was thick as I recalled my barefoot days in Wenzhou. My toes remembered the hot earth, the running, the freedom on summer days. In our fenced-in backyard, we'd take turns holding a perforated Tupperware container while chasing the tiny flashing lights with cupped palms.

When it grew dark, our mother called us back into the kitchen with promises of something sweet. One of her favorite fruits was the giant Korean pear with thick coarse skin like a brown paper bag. In a hushed voice, she'd tell us to feel how juicy and heavy the fruit was; they were two for five dollars in Flushing. She had a habit of telling us the cost of food, even though we had no context for whether the price was reasonable or not. Fruit and meat were a rarity when she was our age. We didn't understand her hardship, but we didn't need to, we knew enough to be ashamed of our luxuries and to indulge her. We passed the fruit around, lifted it up dramatically. Henry used it as a dumbbell and pretended to weight-lift with it. I rubbed it as if it were the bald head of a Buddha. Jill held it with both hands, an offering, and passed it back to our mother.

With a small knife, she peeled the rough mustardy skin. Clear juice ran down the serrated knife and into the creased web between her thumb and index finger. We watched wide-eyed, as the speckled coarse skin came off in a single long spiral. It curled and sat like a phantom pear; a shell without a body, so used to being the shape it had always been that it retained the memory. The moist white flesh glistened as she cut it into eighths. Distribution of food wasn't by age, but by hierarchy and importance. The first piece went to my stepfather, followed by Henry, Jill, and then me. I knew not to ask for seconds and instead chose to put my hands between the seat and my butt.

"Just two bites, Mei Mei," my mother pleaded. I had eaten my piece too quickly, but Jill hadn't touched hers. I eyed her slices.

Jill squeezed her sliver of pear between two fingers. She sat with her entire body on the chair, legs tucked under her slouching torso. She was small for her age, and my mother fretted over her eating. Years later, I will wonder if one of the reasons she ate so poorly was because I ate so well. My mother's obsession with keeping me in line taught her how to be the daughter my mother always wanted. She heeded her words, and grew pliant and obedient. I was an extension of our mother that she wanted to control, but it was my sister who molded herself into a pleasing image of goodness and filial piety, into what our mother needed.

"Another piece?" she asked my stepfather.

My mother expected me to understand the delicate dynamic of our situation: I was the child of her last marriage and I should tread lightly so as not to offend my new benefactors. I was to be seen and not heard, I was to do well in school, but not better than her other children. I was never to outshine them in any way.

Growing up, being good didn't consist of eating my vegetables, making my bed, or doing well in school; it was accepting a new reality, knowing when to be helpful, when to stay out of my stepfather's and Henry's way, when to disappear. In exchange for my mother bringing me to the States, I had signed an unspoken contract, promising this and more. And in the moment, it meant looking on and knowing not to ask for seconds.

My stepfather shook his head, and my mother eyed me for a long second before sticking the knife in the last piece and pointing it in my direction. I lowered my gaze and then pulled the wedge gently off the sharp tip.

———

I never thought to question the type of work my parents did. For years, I listened to my parents talk about their "gong chong," *factory*, which made "yi fu," *clothes*. I knew it was manual, labor-intensive, and that they worked ten-to-fourteen-hour days. I knew it was loud, dirty, and there was no AC during the hot summers. I knew my mother's back and shoulder still hurt her from the years she'd spent bent over a sewing machine and that every night she soaked in a bath to relieve the pain. I knew my parents could take Sundays off sometimes, but not everyone was so lucky. I sensed rather than understood that there was a lot to complain about, but even more to be grateful for.

It wasn't until much later that I began to realize what a factory was, and even more complicated, what a sweatshop was. If you look up the word *factory*, you'll find two definitions, the first being "a station where factors reside and trade." The word first appeared in the 1500s and referred to brokers, people who enact or transact business for others. In Latin, *factor* simply means "doer." Over time, the word began to have a second meaning: a good or service (such as land, labor, or capital) used in the process of production.

The factory system was first adopted by the British at the beginning of the Industrial Revolution. It came to America by way of mills, and appealed to young, unskilled women. The term *mill girls* was used to describe women, generally fifteen to thirty years old, who worked in the cotton factories. In the early 1820s, Lowell Mills Girls, mostly unmarried daughters of New England farmers looking for an opportunity to be free of fathers and husbands, were the first wave of textile workers. They moved into boarding-houses that emphasized the importance of education, providing nightly curfews, meals, and the occasional social. It was a safe option that appealed to both parents and daughters.

In the depression of the 1830s, when the otherwise decent wages were reduced by 15 percent, the Lowell Mills Girls protested, "turned out," as they used to say. Their walkouts for fairer wages led to opportunities for Irish and Italian immigrants. By the end of the Depression, factories belonged to both women and immigrants. Unions began to form for safer working conditions, fair wages, and comprehensive benefits. Strikes brought opportunities for Polish, Chinese, and Mexican immigrants eager to work, while allowing factories to keep operating. When they left for better opportunities or to join unions, new immigrants took their place. They were people who spoke no English or who, because of their undocumented status, could not gather or unionize, and could not afford to attract attention.

The U.S. Department of Labor defines a sweatshop as any factory that violates two or more labor laws such as those on wages, benefits, working hours, and child labor. Anti-sweatshop advocates go further, to say that beyond following the laws, which are weak in some countries and have loopholes in others, a factory must pay a living wage in safe working conditions, agree to reasonable work hours, provide sick leave and maternity leave, and allow workers to organize.

After 1965, three businesses emerged among the Chinese population in New York as a direct effect of the immigration policy that abolished the National Origins Formula, a largely discriminatory system that restricted immigrants from Asia and southern and eastern Europe. The policy gave opportunities to new immigrants arriving to work, and then start their own restaurant, laundry, or garment business. Anthropologist Bernard P. Wong

wrote that the increase in garment businesses gave the influx of
women arriving to the city the opportunity to work. Since sewing was a common skill for women, it was considered a turnkey
situation for growth. Similar to the sweatshops of the Lower East
Side, which started almost a hundred years earlier along with the
influx of Jewish, Italian, and eastern European immigrants, Chinese immigrants grew their own network of laborers through kin
and community.

There were two methods used in garment production. The
first was the whole-garment method, by which each worker did
all the tasks to complete a garment. The other method, the one
my parents used, was the assembly line, dividing responsibility
for each part of the garment. The assembly line or section-work
method was more common, controlled overall quality, and ensured continuity when workers turned over.

Most garment factories and sweatshops were contracting
firms, as the original definition of the word *factor* intended. They
had more orders during high season, cut workers during low
season, and depended on the needs of the market. According to
Wong, most Chinese-owned garment factories in New York were
relatively small, not like the behemoth factories in Asia now, and
ranged from forty to sixty people. Although many of them were
registered as corporations, most of them were owned by family
members or relatives, like my family.

My initial understanding of the workers was from my
mother's harsh voice. Her tone taught my half siblings and me
to both fear and respect their lives and the hard labor they did.
In the Chinese community, we were apprehensive of the cruelty

of chance and luck, even though we didn't fully understand it. The power employers had over undocumented workers remained a danger that everyone understood, but no one wanted to hear: the vulnerability, the lack of opportunity, the inability to protest poor conditions or to unionize. The difficulty wasn't always in finding another under-the-table job, it was in finding one that didn't exploit the same system, one that treated people with decency and compassion.

—

The people my mother came in contact with were limited in number, but she cared about appearances and saving face. That was especially the case with extended family, including my stepfather's immediate relatives. Like most Taiwanese nationalists, they believed Taiwan to be independent of mainland China, and their bitterness toward mainlanders came from their shared history and their inability to fully claim independence. After Japan handed over Taiwan at the end of World War II, the Republic of China (ROC), led by Chiang Kai-shek, was granted administrative control over Taiwan. When it became clear that he was losing the civil war in China, Taiwan became his home base. And it was there that he imposed martial law and set in motion the forty-eight-year period called the White Terror. The violent suppression led to the arrest, torture, and death of thousands of civilians for their real or perceived opposition. The animosity between Taiwan and China lasted generations, often flaring up from China's refusal to acknowledge Taiwan's independence. Tension remained between Taiwanese and Chinese immigrants wherever they migrated, including New York City.

On one hand, Taiwanese and Chinese immigrants were more alike than any of the other minorities in the city, sharing similar language and culture, but on the other hand, news, politics, and history from their respective homelands got in the way of true amity. News traveled in the papers, on cable TV, and in person. The only way through the prejudice was by building personal relationships. In New York City, large pockets of Chinese-speaking communities were scattered in Queens and Brooklyn: Flushing, Chinatown, and Sunset Park. Taiwanese immigrants tended to look down on mainlanders. Their general view was that mainlanders were uneducated xiang xia zen, country folk, who couldn't think for themselves and lived under Communist rule. It didn't matter whether or not my mother was aware of or attuned to the hostility of her in-laws, but it was her reality once she married my stepfather.

When I think of my stepfather, I hear the round, rich Taiwanese accent that my half siblings also have. I see his flushed red face at our large dining room table, Taiwanese newspaper unfolded before him, a drink at his wrist. Sometimes I can see the gray roots coming through his dyed hair. His father passed away years before I came to the United States, and his mother, like many other elders, moved in with her children. Ama, "grandmother" in Taiwanese, had a permanent room in our house, and she came to live with us for weeks and months at a time.

Filial piety was strong on both sides of our family, but trouble was there from the beginning. Ama was especially passive-aggressive. As a way of showing her true feelings, she would criticize my mother to my stepfather while my mother was within hearing distance. Other times, she'd ask him to relay a message to my mother while she was sitting next to her. My stepfather didn't think much of the treatment, except to say it was childish and would eventually get better, and to just play along until then. They, his mother and sisters, just had to get used to my mother and me. That's how he staved off mini-wars.

Following their mother's example, my stepfather's two sisters looked at my mother as if she still had mud from the streets of China on her face. To them, my mother was a factory worker who somehow won their brother over with her pretty face and damsel-in-distress story. My mother teetered between trying too hard for their approval and ignoring them completely, unable to find a way to please them. It didn't take long for her to realize there was no way to gain their approval, so she adjusted. She kept her kids and husband close but shied away from family events.

For most of my childhood, my stepgrandmother lived with my stepaunt and we would visit them every other weekend. When we arrived at her house—a larger and nicer house than ours—my presence alone was an insult. That my mother would dare bring me, the product of another marriage, to *their* gatherings was a snub, a disregard for their respectable family. My mother was so low-class she didn't even have basic etiquette.

"It's not right," she said to my stepfather on the drive home. "She's my daughter, I'll bring her wherever I want."

She watched me closely at their house, aware of every word spoken to me and every word spoken about me. They mumbled about us in Taiwanese, which my mother was getting better at deciphering. "No one can treat my daughter that way," she fumed on another car ride home. I didn't understand her anger or bitterness, or what made that day different from all the rest, but I was pleased. The shift made me feel a part of the family for the first time. I savored the feeling until our garage door came into view.

Small cutting insults between my mother and Ama and my stepaunts ensured that every gathering was an unpleasant one. Escalation was slow, but tension was constant. Finally, my mother said she would not go to Sunday dinners any longer, and if she didn't go, none of her children would go either. Ama would not get to see her grandkids. On and off, the war waged. My stepfather stayed the frustrated mediator. For months, we'd all stay home, my dedicated stepfather taking trips alone. Our mother's lip stayed in a hard line as we ate dinner without him. After a long winter, Ama asked about my mother and my stepfather relayed the message. It was a sign that she was willing to play nice. It'd be rude of my mother to decline the invitation. She was satisfied that she had proven her point, and then she took Henry and Jill to the following Sunday dinner, but left me at home.

—

Two of my cousins immigrated to New York City around the time I fully assimilated to elementary school. Our family rarely went to visit my aunt, but we did soon after she brought her kids over from China. It was a joyous occasion, like the party my parents threw when I first arrived. For years, my aunt and uncle saved and worked overtime so that this reunion would be possible. It was painful but common for parents to leave China without their children. Grandparents, aunts and uncles, friends and neighbors stepped in to take them. In exchange, money was sent home monthly to cover costs. Often it was enough to improve the lives of the children and those relatives. The separation allowed parents to settle in to their new American surroundings unburdened. They slept in tight quarters with other newly immigrated workers, often on floors, on thin mattresses. It was easier to find housing, to work impossibly long days, and to save money without a family. There was no room for children, no money for childcare, and those factors overrode any sentimentality over separation.

Separation may have been commonplace, but having your kids with you was a rite of passage, a reinforced incentive on a road toward prosperity and the American dream. To have your children with you was a talked-about privilege. I didn't remember my cousins; we were children from different worlds by then. I vaguely recognized the girl. She was a year older and the boy was a year younger than me, and we had grown up playing together as toddlers. They had a startled, fresh-off-the-boat meekness—their frightened expressions so familiar and undisguised, it hurt my eyes. Their clothing was coarse, cheap, poorly made, and screamed Made in China, and ran large over their thin, undernourished frames. Being around them made me feel self-conscious, made me remember who I was when I arrived—the same un-Americanness that kids at school made fun of, the Chinese part of myself I thought I'd eradicated.

I walked around my aunt's cramped one-bedroom, pacing, listening to my mother praise how much space they had. Was she joking? I couldn't believe she was saying the place was nice. All the furniture was plastic, except for the kitchen table and the bed. The wobbly tables and plastic chairs were uncomfortable and cheap. The floor had vintage-looking tiles that had been bleached until they were a different color, and still looked unclean. The bathroom had plastic basins in the tub, dark spots on the ceiling, and baggy underwear hanging over the curtain rod. It smelled of moisture and mildew.

Though we were all immigrants, my extended family led more difficult lives. It was painfully obvious. They worked as hard as my parents, but they had less and saved hardly anything at all.

"Do you know English?" I asked my cousins when it was clear there was nothing else to do.

My cousins shook their heads in unison. They looked alike; the girl had a short pixie cut that made her features more delicate, and the boy was all bones.

"How about Mandarin?" I pressed. I was not used to having more than other kids, and I chose the moment as an opportunity to gloat.

They shook their heads again.

"Do you know how to read?" I taunted.

"We're going to school soon," the older one said, speaking up and putting a protective arm around her brother.

I nodded at her. "It's hard, but you can learn."

She squeezed her brother. He didn't pull away and seemed to come out of his shell a bit. I looked over at Henry and Jill playing by themselves and staying close to our parents. They had no interest in talking to our cousins or to me.

"You can't wear the same clothes from China to school every day. They'll make fun of you."

"Why not?" the younger one whispered so lightly I could barely hear him. He seemed more affected by the situation than his sister. "This is America," I stated simply, and then added quietly, "Ask your ma to buy some."

We looked over at my aunt. They hadn't seen their mother in years, but even at their age they knew there was no money. It should have been enough to make it to America, but they would soon realize it was not. They would need school supplies, new clothes, a separate room to grow up in. They would compare themselves with kids in school who were more fortunate than them, kids that learned English faster, parents that had more than their parents. We were silent, too aware of the impossibilities of our lives.

At least they remembered their parents, I thought. At least they had only been separated for two years and not five like my mother and me. At least they didn't have a new family when they got here. Even though I knew the struggle they would face, I felt longing and something close to envy. I looked at the way they huddled together—at least they had each other.

I decided I liked them. I grabbed the girl's hand and tried to get in between them. The younger one refused to let go of his sister's hand. I pried his fingers off one by one, his grip tight and white around the knuckle. His face darkened and contorted with each finger I pulled away. When he seemed about to cry,

I looked over at my mother in conversation with my aunt. She would never let me join their family. "Okay, okay, don't cry," I said, letting go.

"Don't think I didn't see that! This is why I never take you anywhere," my mother hissed the moment my aunt turned away. She yanked painfully at my arm as a warning.

Just last week, I had gotten into a bad fight with Henry. Five years younger than me, he outweighed me by about fifteen pounds. Whenever we got into fights, they became wrestling matches, like one of Henry's favorite things on TV, WWE, where we learned about what the Rock was cooking.

He sat on my head, farting. I grew light-headed in the dark crevice of our couch. I felt the hard bottom underneath me and tried to use it as leverage to shift my shoulder blade out from under my brother's weight. When that didn't work, I tried to wrap my legs around his upper body and scissor-kick him off. I sank farther between two cushions. A breathless second passed and I resorted to pinching his rolls of baby fat. It was an endurance game—who would be the first to give in? I was almost ready to muffle a sound of defeat when I felt the softness of my brother's inverted nipple. I wrapped my thumb and index finger around it and twisted. When he didn't budge, I dug my nails in and twisted again. He rolled off, slow as a sloth. All at once fresh air flooded my lungs and white lights evaporated before my eyes. He ran into the kitchen and left me breathing hard. I had won.

Around 8:00 p.m., headlights pulled into the driveway and

the garage door rolled up. Fighting with my brother meant an automatic beating, so a sense of dread settled in my belly. He was the golden child, the boy heir to my stepfather's line, and I could never win.

The aroma of white rice filled the second floor and my stomach growled. I needed to find a way to get out of trouble. I had an idea! I would go on a hunger strike. I lay on the carpet in the room I shared with Jill and put my hand on my flat belly. My aunt once told me that if you still had a flat belly after eating, it meant you could keep eating. When you were full, your belly would protrude and refuse to suck in. She laughed when she told me this, but I didn't get the joke.

Voices were coming up through the carpet. I closed my eyes and imagined what they were eating. Sweet and sour spareribs? Scallion and ginger steamed fish? Fried and salted shrimp? Chinese okra? I sat on my bed, then got off and remade it so it was neat and smooth. My mother hated creases, messes, or any sort of imperfection. I cleaned my desk and then wished I had my book bag. Did I have time to sneak downstairs and get it now without being noticed? I put my ear flat against the carpet again and listened to the sound of their muffled conversations, chopsticks against porcelain plates. My empty stomach made another gnarly sound as I shifted.

Half an hour passed, then my mother's quick steps traveled up the stairs. I got up off the carpet, pulled the hair out of my face, and sat on the chair in front of my desk. Before I could say anything, she wordlessly yanked my upper arm with enough force to pull me off my seat. I held on to the back of the chair with my free arm until the chair tilted and collapsed. I clawed at it as she dragged me out of the room. When it was clear she was too strong for me, I made my body limp and heavy, letting my thighs drag ribbons on the carpet.

Henry stood shirtless in the hall, wearing a pair of long sport shorts. His upper body resembled the laughing Maitreya Buddha, with breasts and a comically large belly. His skin was milky and smooth except for the bruises around his right nipple. Two greenish hues, like strokes from a watercolor brush, marred his chest, next to another blunt, purple bruise.

"Look at this!" she fumed. "His father houses you, feeds you, sends you to school, and this is what you do to his son? How are you going to pay for this? How!"

I had a whole speech prepared, a short but concise relay of events, but I found I could not speak. His bruises were worse than I'd thought and I had no comparable wounds, no defense for the angry marks on his body. I had only wanted a turn with the remote, but Henry hogged all our TV time. Even I knew the reasoning sounded small. I looked up at her face. Was my stepfather really mad at me?

"You're his older sister, you're supposed to take care of him. Ah yo ah! I was wrong to bring you to America. I've been cursed to give birth to a child like you."

I burst into tears, and my mother looked like she was ready to cry too.

Henry turned to her and they stared at each other for a moment. With a frustrated headshake, she turned and went back downstairs without another word.

"Are you crying?" he asked me, and then gleefully shouted, "I win!"

I watched as he walked back down the stairs bare-chested. It had never been a contest: we were not equal. No one cared if I starved myself, and there was no amount of self-punishment that would match any suffering he went through. I felt it then, my insignificance against his importance, and I could not hold back my anguish. That feeling gripped me again as my two cousins inched together. The girl whispered something into her brother's ear and he calmed. I looked over at Henry. He was on his new Game Boy. Jill sat close to him, watching him play. I wondered if there was something missing in the way I felt about them. For a fleeting moment, I saw that there could have been another way with my family.

Even then, I knew my cousins' lives were not interchangeable with my half siblings' or with mine. It was one of the reasons my mother's fears seemed both real and surreal, close and yet a fleeting concern. Our middle-class lives were protected and full of potential compared to theirs, but from her point of view, it could all go away. As I looked out at their inevitable hardships, I felt a hunger. I felt like I always did: this was not enough.

My mother's rags-to-riches story was as much hard work as it was good fortune, but it was the fortune that everyone saw. My father's sister sponsored her to the United States years before any of her siblings, and her marriage to my stepfather was another strike of fortune. My stepfather was an immigrant as well, but he came from an upper-middle-class background in Taiwan. They had family and resources, even if there were still restrictions on types of opportunity for Taiwanese men.

While my mother was able to fly to Wenzhou and bring me to the United States, most of my extended family spent years and countless resources finding their way to America. They had a typical narrative: they left Wenzhou for Hong Kong, and lived there for years until an opportunity to emigrate to the United States appeared. They had few connections besides my mother. When they arrived in New York, like so many others in the country then, large debts awaited them. Immediately, the women started at the sweatshops and the men did manual work, loading and unloading deliveries from trucks for grocery stores, restaurants, laundry services, and the garment industries. It took years, capital, and new connections for other prospects to appear.

Many of my relatives depended on the Chinese community and the intricate network and channels of trade. Often they led all the way back to our home province and to the people they knew there. Money was sent back for kids and elders, while rare food and sometimes medicine was smuggled back to New York. The trade, small and large, created demand, and then markets for new business in both countries. In the 1990s and onward, businesses such as wholesaling grew in Wenzhou and surrounding cities, exporting manufactured items like plastic furniture, toys for kids and schools, leatherwork, and knockoff luxury accessories. The network grew large enough to support families on both ends, providing a resource to lean on for multiple generations.

China has caught up, but in the 1970s and '80s class mobility was possible only in the United States. Almost everyone that came stayed, stranded in limbo among hundreds of thousands of other Chinese immigrants fighting for housing, jobs, and shortcuts to assimilation and profit. The ones who arrived like my mother, aunts, and uncles never fully integrated. They simply needed to make a living, and then if they were fortunate, a better living. The goal was to accumulate wealth. Education, learning English, and assimilation were left to their kids, and depending on their legal status and how they did in school, they either went off to college or began working with family and friends. Many ended up in family businesses out of necessity, out of opportunity, out of obligation.

3

Life-changing occurrences should feel like they have more gravity than they do. Like many Chinese families above a certain income, we had a live-in maid who cooked, cleaned, and looked after the children. The ah-yis, aunties, as we called them, never lasted long and no one in our family was surprised when the latest one was fired. My mother announced she was gone when there was no dinner on the table.

Maids lasted weeks, months, and—on two occasions—more than a year. Sometimes we got to say goodbye, other times they disappeared without a trace. My mother had her reasons for getting rid of them: laziness, incompetence, bad cooking, or a combination of those offenses. A few times, she suspected them of stealing. This time the food was too salty and she was eating too much. When there wasn't a maid to make my half siblings' beds, clean my parents' master bedroom, do the laundry, take my parents' clothes to the dry cleaner, sweep and mop the wood floors, vacuum the upstairs carpet, wash the dishes, prep for dinner, and a hundred other tasks, it fell on me.

At first, my mother would make an effort to look for a replacement in the local Flushing paper. In the meantime, she told me, I was in charge. "You are qie qie," she said in Mandarin, pausing for effect. *Older sister* echoed in my head. "Henry and Jill will follow your lead."

Every day I picked Henry and Jill up from school, made snacks, watched over them while they worked on their homework, practiced piano, and chipped away at a long list of chores. I made sure they took their baths, while simultaneously cleaning my parents' room, making their bed, cleaning the bathrooms, washing the dishes left from the morning, and prepped for dinner.

At the age of thirteen, every morning before I left for school, I reported to my mother for an extra list of chores: wax the couch, Windex the windows and mirrors, scrub the deck, wash out the trash cans, dust the blinds, organize my half siblings' books and toys. Helping out at home soon became ying gai de, *expected.* According to my mother, I was old enough that we no longer needed a maid. What was she raising me for? Whenever I protested, I got her side-eye. *Do you think you would be here if it wasn't for me? Do you know how lucky you are?* She didn't want to hear excuses about my own homework or studying; helping the family came first.

She was meticulous and missed nothing, and I was no match for the kind of criticism she had for maids. A long string of complaints started as soon as she came home. If she didn't like how I had done something, which was the majority of the time, I'd have to do it over. Mop the floor twice, clean out the fridge again, dust the display cabinets a second time, vacuum the master bedroom, and wax her shoes a third time. Soon it didn't matter that I had it better than half the immigrants who arrived in New York. In the midst of hand-washing my mother's bloody underwear, ironing my stepfather's shirts, and yelling at Henry to go take his bath for the third time, I didn't care if I was the luckiest of kids without a father. I only wanted to get away from my mother, to not be designated the substitute maid. I resented everything she had given me, wished I could give it all back, and at the same time felt the weight of all that I owed her.

When Henry sprayed water out of the tub and onto the mat and refused to get out, I became domineering, my voice raising with annoyance. Why was their father alive and mine dead? How was it my fault that my father died? If I wasn't sitting with Jill while she practiced piano, she'd start lying on the bench, playing songs she already knew instead of practicing songs she had learned in the past week. When she was done, Henry mocked me. "*It's your turn. Play the piano, Henry. It's your turn.*" I wanted to wrestle him down and slam his face into the piano keys until he shut up, until we could trade places, until we were just brother and sister. Instead, I shouted the only threat I had, "I'll call Mom if you don't stop!"

"*I'll call Mom, I'll call Mom,*" he sang. He ran around the living room fresh from his bath and naked, his pale belly hanging.

If I could get through on the phone, my mother could get him to practice, but if I couldn't, I would be the one in trouble at the end of the day. She didn't want excuses, just results.

A maid's ad in the local Chinese newspaper always worked, but salaries had gone up and maids wanted certain rights, like a day off once a week to be with their own family. Even with room and food, they were asking for $1,000 a month. My mother grumbled at how things were changing and put off hiring, and I steeled myself against what it would mean for me.

My life rapidly took a turn so that between 2:30 and 8:00 p.m., there was only time for the long list of chores, and babysitting Henry and Jill. After my parents came home, I helped my mother in the kitchen, prepping the meat I had defrosted, the vegetables I had washed, the rice I cleaned and started in the rice cooker. After dinner, cleanup was on my own. I washed the dishes, scrubbed the pots and pans, wiped down the counters and kitchen table, and swept and mopped the kitchen floor. Then I went around the house, cleaning up toys on the floor and drawing the curtains.

It was bedtime when I was done cleaning up, and there was no time left for homework or prepping for exams. My mother wasn't concerned about my grades the way she was for my half siblings'. She had come so far in life with just a sixth-grade education from rural Wenzhou. No one in her family had much of an education, and if that was good enough for her, it was good enough for me.

My stepfather had a different childhood, and had attended college in Taiwan. His education led him to understand the opportunities abroad in the United States and, later, to establish his own business. His English was impeccable and his slightly European accent more sophisticated than that of most Chinese immigrants, who learned the language out of necessity. His upbringing meant my parents constantly worried about how well Henry and Jill did in school.

I did my reading walking to school, finished homework during the few minutes between classes and during lunch. When I was desperate, I snuck homework in during class time when teachers weren't paying attention. I grew painfully conscious of my dropping grades, and the confused and then disappointed reactions from my teachers. My frustration grew as weeks turned into months.

Unlike my half siblings, I loved participating in school and getting good grades. My desire for approval and normalcy had long transferred to how I performed in the classroom. I soaked up the attention and potential my teachers saw in me. Their praise lifted me, made me feel like just another student, made me forget about the chores waiting at home, the fear of my mother getting home before they were done. There was hope of acceptance where being a stepchild at home was fukunang, *impossible*.

———

One night, a couple of months after my mother fired the last maid, I waited until my eyes adjusted to the darkness outside my room. It was 10:30 when my bare toes met the smooth, forbidden wood floors of the living room. I could tell from the light under my parents' bedroom that they were still up, watching Taiwanese sitcoms. I could always tell the slight lilt and tonal difference be-

tween mainland and Taiwanese Mandarin, the cultural gap between my mother and stepfather.

With each step, I grew more aware that bedtime was at ten
o'clock and what I was doing was against the rules. There would
be a beating if I got caught, but I settled down cross-legged in
front of the coffee table. The soft hum of the house kept me
company as I opened up my five-subject notebook and pulled
out my Spanish workbook. My Spanish teacher was known to
make students stand up in class and hold a conversation using
new vocabulary words. The silence in the classroom was always
humiliating and terrifying. I was determined to be prepared
this time. Staying up late was the only solution with my impossible chore list.

I'd been downstairs for a good twenty minutes when the hairs
on my neck rose. From the corner of my eye, I saw my mother's
powder-pink robe, quilted polyester grazing the floor as she leaned
down toward me. Her hot breath sent shudders down my spine.

"Ni ze la jou nie?" she hissed in my ear. *What are you doing?*

In a panic, I slammed my textbook shut and started stuff-
ing my notebook and textbooks into my book bag. I stood up
and put my bag back in the dining room, next to Henry's and
Jill's book bags. She trailed behind me, calmly waiting for me to
come up with an excuse. How could I explain myself? Why did
I need to explain that I needed to do my homework? Why was
my education expendable? The more I thought about my situation, the angrier I grew in my justification. I actually wanted to be
good at school, unlike Henry or Jill. There was no sound except
my breathing. Her pink slippers muted her footsteps behind me.

Sweat rose to my upper lip and I turned to the adjoining kitchen. My hands were clammy and useless. The bottom of my feet perspired on the cool tiled floor as the square footage of the kitchen shrank. I wasn't ready to face her, but it was the end of the line. There was nowhere left to go.

I grabbed a tumbler from the cabinet and pressed the water button on the fridge. A cool stream splashed the base and I could feel the liquid move through the glass.

"What do you think you're doing?" she repeated.

I turned before the water had filled the glass.

"I—I'm drinking water," I said, buying time.

Her eyes narrowed and I realized she thought I was being smart with her, talking back. I opened my mouth to explain, but before I was able to, there was a loud smack and a sharp ring in my ear. Slowly, I brought my face and hot cheek back around. Then I put my hands out in front of me and shoved her.

"Hue. Wou ja wou ja." She sneered. *All right, all right. That's great.*

"I just wanted to do my homework. I never have time—"

Crack. The sound echoed through the spotless kitchen and the same burn, deeper this time, spread across the left side of my face. My hands had a life of their own; I had no control over them. I watched as they lengthened in front of me again, pushing her with enough force that her hundred-pound body rocked and a strand of hair fell around her temple.

"Hitting your mother now, huh? You're a real grown-up!"

"I just want time to do my homew—" I said, my throat so heavy with tears it ached to swallow them down.

"Let's see what *he* has to say about this . . ." She was gone, her robe a pink cape trailing behind her.

I stood staring at my hands. They had betrayed me and I wanted to sever them from my body, make what had happened an involuntary act I could deny. The long fingers and bony knuckles that resembled my mother's held steady. There was no trace of remorse on them.

Water had spilled from the glass onto the tiled floor. I couldn't remember when it happened, but there it was, a clear wet blotch on the clean surface I had swept and mopped only an hour ago. An hour felt like a lifetime. I was a different person then. Now I was a child that struck her mother, a monster.

A sliver of moon crept in through the window in the kitchen; spring crickets sounded in the distance. I wanted to crawl into the pitch-blackness and go to sleep, hide my shame before anyone found out, before what would happen next. Raising a hand against my mother was infinitely worse than talking back, worse than fighting with Henry, worse than stealing from her purse, worse than calling her "Mom" in public, worse than anything I had ever done. The seconds passed as I stood there, afraid to move and unsure of what to do. Cautiously, I made my way up the stairs, pausing every few steps to listen and wait out the creaks. Just as I sat down on my bed, the door slammed loudly against the wall, and my stepfather stormed in. He seemed startled, suddenly aware of himself and where he was. He went into my half siblings' room regularly, but never visited mine. He left me to my mother, as he promised all those years ago, and his presence was new to both of us.

"You ... Get out!" he said in English. He was breathing hard and his hand pointed out the door. It could have been the remains of the beers he had for dinner or a reaction to what my mother just told him, but his face was flushed. "I don't want you sleeping on the same floor as this family."

"Where should I go?"

"I don't care!" he shouted, already at the top of the stairs, guardian of the upper floor. There was something unapproachable in his face. He looked like the angry, red-faced Menshen, one of the door gods who guarded and protected homes from evil. We had statues of the three door gods sitting on top of the cabinet in the living room, their fierce eyes and enraged faces watching over us. Once, I asked my mother why we kept them around. She said they were mean-looking for a reason: to ward off evil. My stepfather had the same stance, the same face. "Go! *Go!*"

He was a nice, nonconfrontational man, a generous and doting if sometimes absent father. He was the pushover parent, the good guy who would sway under the pressure of his kids' bartering and begging. He signed mediocre report cards, paid for class trips, and provided a generous allowance for Henry and Jill. He gave hugs. I couldn't process the shift, the way he was sending me away. By the time he finished speaking, something had been revealed and taken away in the same moment—this invisible strand of hope that tethered me to the dynamic of the four of them. I had been harboring hope since I joined his family that he might one day be as warm and generous to me as his own kids. I thought I could win over his affection, but now that dream was shattered, gone before I could even admit the longing to myself, gone before

I could hold and tend to the hope, gone before I could try to make it known.

I got up off my bed. This man in my room was a stranger. I called him Baba, but he was not my father, he was just the man who married my mother and allowed her child from a previous marriage to live under the same roof as his family. I hadn't wanted to believe it, but it was just like she said. He was the door god showing me his wrath. I headed back down the stairs, through the living room for a third time that night, and then farther, to the lowest level of the house.

The basement air was refreshing against my hot face. I didn't bother to turn the light on. I knew exactly where he wanted me to go. Even in the dark, I could make out the twin bed in the maid's room. The mattress was stripped bare. I curled up into the farthest corner of the bed, exhausted, my face damp against the scratchy mattress. This was where I belonged now.

—

The next day, after my parents came home from work and we had dinner as a family like we always did, my mother handed me a navy Delta plane ticket. The confidence I'd worked up evaporated as I stared at it. The flight was to Xi'an International Airport, leaving in just two days. She didn't need to say anything, I understood.

If you keep fighting with Henry, we will have to send you back to China.

Keep talking back—see what happens.

If you don't listen, we'll send you back to China.

Be stubborn, just wait and see.

The threats ran on a loop in my brain. Same old warning turned stale, but here it was, a reality. How did it happen? Why hadn't I prevented it from happening? I'd been banking on the fact that she was my mother and I was her daughter. That truth tied us together like no other relationship, didn't it? I trusted that her long and arduous journey to bring me to America had meant something. I trusted *her*, my mother, to keep me at her side. I couldn't grasp this life change, this sudden reality, but the ticket was in my hand and everything had been arranged.

4

The tallest Chinese man I ever saw picked me up at Xi'an Xianyang International Airport. He must have been well over six feet tall, and he held a torn piece of paper with my name on it in Chinese: 瞿娜. We didn't shake hands or touch, he simply nodded and asked for my carry-on. After a twenty-four-hour flight, which included a complicated transfer in Beijing, I was exhausted and numb.

I trailed behind him, slow to follow, reluctant to leave the airport and worried I wouldn't know my way back. *Back home.* My chest tightened at the thought. I had been sent back to China to live with strangers. I looked over at the carry-on suitcase; it had everything called home now. What if this stranger took off with my suitcase and left me in a dirt parking lot? Who would help me then? It hit me that no one in the world knew where I was at that moment. I was a speck of dust on the ground of a parking lot more than seven thousand miles from Queens. He had long strides. I picked up my pace.

Sending you to Nie Nie would be a reward, my mother had told me. She didn't want my grandparents to spoil me, so she arranged for a retired couple, parents of one of her factory workers, to take me in for a monthly fee. It felt surreal to be off the plane and in China. The natural sunlight felt out of place, harsher on my bare skin. The dirt was a yellower color here, more vibrant and more granular than sand. The seasons had changed and it felt too hot for early May. It was midday here and midnight back in New York. I squinted up at the blazing sun, exhausted.

It was always in unexpected moments that I thought about my father. He was a face I could not remember, a parent I did not know, a caregiver I wish I had. I turned to him like others turned to God, a light I could pray to. I had kept it together the entire flight, but now getting in a beat-up car, in a part of China I'd never been, everything crystalized amid the arid dirt, I lost it.

The world had cracked open and I had fallen in. The weight of his death hit me in waves as the old man lifted my cheap carry-on suitcase into the trunk of his car. *This is what happens to fatherless children*, my mother always warned me. I swallowed the dryness in my throat, the taste of ash, the echo of her voice. We drove in silence. The closer we got to the center of the city, the dustier it became and the more things felt permanent. There was no air-conditioning in the car. I rolled down the window the rest of the way and took in the sound and smell of Xi'an. The air was gritty and the smell was unfamiliar, like cured meat and soot.

"Chong Chun." He nodded as we passed through a tunnel.

Traffic was at a standstill under the Xi'an City Wall. I looked behind us and watched the length of the wall extend as far as the eye could see on both sides. Xi'an was an ancient, overpopulated city surrounded by the wall. Built during the Ming dynasty, it was the oldest and best-preserved wall in China. The city likes its white flour. Every street corner food vendor sold fried buns and spicy flat noodles, a provincial specialty I did not like. It was not the China I remembered.

The elderly couple were polite and soft-spoken. Retirees content with their lives, they had a small circle of friends in the surrounding building complexes. At five o'clock every morning, they rose. For breakfast, they ate a couple of small white buns each, washed down with hot water. For special mornings, they fried the buns and had them with tea. At noon, each ate a bowl of flat noodles composed mostly of hot sauce. Then, for dinner, they had a snack or nothing at all. Their diet was an adjustment for me and I was constipated immediately upon arrival. The chili oil made it into every dish and was too heavy for my palate. Every afternoon, the tall old man would read the paper and hang out in his office, and the old woman would mend or wash something for the apartment. They played Go or visited with friends. Usually their days ended early, and they went to bed before nine.

They were not expecting to raise a teenager. I called them Nai Nai and Yie Yie out of courtesy, and they introduced me as their granddaughter or the daughter of a friend. I was reminded of the shame I carried in New York, of the way my mother told me to call her Aunt in public where people might know her. Now I was living another lie, another scarlet shame. Even as a fourteen-year-old, I could tell they didn't want any problems. They may have wondered why any parent would send their child back when so many couldn't get their children to America, but they never asked.

—

My mother was generous when we were apart. She called every two weeks, just like she did when she left me in Wenzhou with my grandparents. It was an easy habit to slip back into. "Fifty dollars is a lot of money," my mother told me over the phone when we spoke a few days later. "Are you happy? Fifty dollars a month! I got him to agree."

The irony was that Henry and Jill had been receiving fifty-dollar allowances for years now, but I had to disappear from their lives and move halfway across the world to get what they had.

"Yes," I replied, "great." The distance was a cool rag on a raging wound. It should have made me happy that she actually sounded caring and patient, but instead, her courteous tone made me grit my teeth. It infuriated me. Why did I need to be halfway across the world for her to be nice? But I instinctively bit back my anger and became the obedient daughter overseas. I told her whatever she wanted to hear and let her think she'd made the right decision by sending me here. She was the adult and I was the child. Her calls were lifelines, my chances to convince her that I'd learned my lesson and would behave better.

—

I bought a disposable camera with my allowance and started posing at the entrances of sites like I was on vacation. I never got the hang of asking for directions or reading signs. The pushy commuters mobbing busses made traveling sweaty and frenzied. I visited the Giant Wild Goose Pagoda, Drum Tower of Xi'an, Bell Tower of Xi'an, and the Small Wild Goose Pagoda. I hit all the temples, museums, libraries, bookstores, and markets, exhausting Xi'an's list of things to do. One time, I stumbled on an international bookstore where I found two Jane Austen novels: *Emma* and *Pride and Prejudice*. I read *Emma* in days, and never got through all of *Pride and Prejudice*. A few weeks later, I tried to go back to the same bookstore, but I was never able to find it again.

One of my first class trips in elementary school was to the local library. I received my first library card on that day. My parents weren't readers, and my siblings were five and six years younger and only flipping through picture books, so the library felt like a minor miracle. I remember the joy of finding the American Girl series, a collection of dolls and books I'd seen many times. I had coveted them ever since a classmate brought them in for show-and-tell. I couldn't believe I could borrow the whole Felicity series for free. I had outgrown dolls, and the library was missing two books in the series, but I went back an embarrassing number of times, hoping they would be returned.

We lived only five blocks from the Auburndale library, one of the few places my mother allowed our ai-yis to take us while growing up. I remember borrowing Roald Dahl's *The Witches* and walking into a lamppost on my way home. The children's section took up half the second room in the library, but I moved through the shelves meticulously and efficiently. I wasn't a picky reader: I demolished R. L. Stine's Goosebumps series, Ann M. Martin's Baby-Sitters Club series, and C. S. Lewis's Chronicles of Narnia. When I outgrew the back room, I moved on to the YA section in the front of the library. That's where I started with Sandra Brown's mysteries and suspense novels, and when they were done, I found her romance novels. I missed romance novels the most.

Some evenings, just as the sun was going down at the complex, I would follow the smell of cumin in the air. At any of the three food stalls at the corner of the complex, I would find barbecued meat on a stick: cumin chicken butt, cumin pork, cumin beef, cumin innards. I was on an adventure, a journey to discover the best BBQ in Xi'an. I held on to the belief that I was living out my punishment and that if I behaved—learned my lesson—she'd let me come home.

One weekend, a month into my stay, fake Yie Yie came with me onto the City Wall, which was within walking distance of their apartment complex. He stood as I ran a mile up and then down from where he stood, looking out at the entrance of the city. He peered over street vendors and pedestrians, the upright bicycle riders and overcrowded scooters with families of four and sometimes five, large transportation vehicles sputtering black smoke into the streets over vendors selling produce. As far as the eye could see, corner vendors stood with white buns, noodles, and breakfast food. I wanted to stay up there forever, where the dust and dirt couldn't reach me, where I could see the neatly framed streets below us and breathe clean air for the first time since I arrived. Beyond the wall were valleys and rice paddies, and just past those, I thought I could glimpse the airport where I had landed.

—

By the end of the summer, after three months of living in Xi'an, I thought surely my mother would allow me to return to New York and start eighth grade. I was growing anxious and restless, pacing for days waiting for her next call. I missed my friend Grace. I missed her bubbly handwriting, the Korean bands she talked about, the music she made me listen to, and the conversations that were often about nothing but made me feel normal. There was no way to keep in touch, no way to find out how she was doing. Did she think about me? Were we still friends? Had she found another best friend?

If I closed my eyes, I could smell New York, the particular reek of trash in the summer heat, sidewalks baking until steam rose off them. I could hear the sound of tires meeting asphalt as cars drove by our block at night. I missed taking the bus without being afraid I wouldn't make it home. I missed walking to the Auburndale library, having companions in novels, being able to escape my life. I missed understanding the world I had worked hard to be a part of. The strangeness of my isolation drove me to tell my mother in various ways that I had learned my lesson. I would do chores without complaining now, I wouldn't do my homework or compare myself to my half siblings. In late August, I asked how they were, trying to show her that I cared about them. She said they were fine, and since things seemed to be working out with me in Xi'an, she was going to arrange for me to stay.

"Stay? Here?" I asked, my voice an octave higher than usual.

"There's an expensive boarding school for international kids. American kids. I'm going to have Yie Yie register you." Her words were careful, slightly too airy, as if she had just run up a flight of stairs.

I used to think my mother didn't understand me because she had retrained me to speak only when I was spoken to. The only way to get what I wanted was by waiting, enduring, and not asking for it outright. A woman's life. Sometimes she rewarded my silence with treats or a second serving of food at the dinner table. I thought if I kept my mouth shut about wanting to come home, she'd take me back, and now I was dumbfounded. Why had the rules changed?

"Enrollment is over, but we made a couple of calls and got you in." I could hear the pride in her words as if she'd pulled off something extraordinary. There was hope in her voice. "Ai yo ah, it's such an expensive school!"

"I don't want to stay here," I said, my voice cracking. *Please*, I wanted to beg, *please let me come home.*

"Everyone's doing fine here and it's better if you stay there." Her voice was cold and curt. It told me the topic was not up for debate. "I wish I had the option of going to such a nice school when I was a kid."

I hesitated. How could I seem grateful and still reject the boarding school? "I have to go back to school in New York, I have to go to P.S. 194. *That's* my school!"

"I knew you still had that temper. This is exactly why you're staying there. It's done. So ungrateful! You'll learn. You know enough Chinese and they'll know English."

I swallowed the thick congestion in my throat and realized nothing I said or did now could change her mind. I hated the way my voice betrayed me, the helpless way my face felt hot.

"Wai?" she said after a moment of pause. "This is an expensive call. Talk or let's hang up."

"They speak English?"

"Of course they will. You don't know how hard it was to get you in. I wish you'd be happy about it. Okay? Hand the phone back."

Everything slowed as I passed the phone over to Yie Yie. I watched him nod. My favorite thing in the apartment was the retro rotary phone. I loved the sound it made when dialing, I loved the thick and perfectly coiled cord that stretched to any space in the small two-bedroom apartment. The ivory handle was full and heavy, and even after I could no longer recall the conversations I had, I remembered the weight of it in my hand. It felt sophisticated and out of place in the largely functional apartment.

I could tell from the way they chatted that it wasn't the first time they'd had this conversation. Details had been exchanged on previous calls without my knowledge. It dawned on me then that they had been planning this for weeks, months, maybe the whole time. "She should be with family," he mumbled into the phone.

My heart missed a beat—was he on my side? He was saying he felt I should go back to the States for school! I would take his pity, I realized, I welcomed it. From under my downcast bangs I could only see his long legs and the uneven patches of hair along his calves. His voice held a note of resolve as he glanced over at me.

My mother's high-pitched voice came through the line, giving sharp orders. Yie Yie listened without interrupting. I curled my toes on the floor. The nails needed to be trimmed. Finally, he grunted, and refused to meet my eyes.

"Hao, hao, wuo dong." His gaze stayed on the desk, his head bowed in defeat, and I knew my last hope had died with his consent.

—

The campus was large, gray, and ugly. The bleak, bare-bones school forced me to recognize that I was no longer in the United States. I was entering a Communist classroom setting. My mother had lied when she said there were international students and English-speakers. None of the students were from outside the city, and English was taught only as a foreign language once a week. There were three grades, seventh, eighth, and ninth, with three classes per grade. The principal put me in class 8A and in a dorm room with five other girls. The bunk beds were neatly arranged in rows and there was a designated place for everything: clothes, books, washbasins, towels, and washcloths. Suddenly, I was never alone. All activity was done in groups, by gender or by class.

Our day started with exercises at 6:30 a.m. out in the cement courtyard. Over loudspeakers we were told to bend, touch our toes, twist, and jump for thirty minutes before reporting to the cafeteria for breakfast. From then on, teachers and monitors surrounded and corrected us all day. Their presence felt like policing to me, especially when they came and went so quietly. They reminded me of my mother's presence. My back stiffened as they made their rounds. Long fingernails, hair below chin length, and skirts above the knee never went unnoticed or uncommented on.

With passable speaking Mandarin and about two years' worth of reading and writing comprehension from Sunday Chinese school in Flushing, I could barely understand what was being asked of me. Learning Chinese was easier in China, but catching up to eighth-grade reading and writing levels was, as my mother often put it, fukunang. I couldn't read the questions on exams, never mind figure out how to respond in Chinese. Another complication was that I had been learning Traditional Chinese, the Taiwanese standard, but all the textbooks were in Simplified Chinese, the Chinese standard. The unlikelihood of overcoming my situation, and the shame of what it meant to be there, a reminder of my mother's abandonment, left me little room to fit in, or the heart to try.

—

A month in, I learned that trying or not trying made little difference to my progress. I was failing every class, except English. I gave up studying Chinese and wrote in my journal most days. The more insecure and lost I felt, the more I acted out. I started saying I didn't need to learn Chinese because I was going back to America, that the school was old and the systems were antiquated, and no one was going to understand my classmates' heavily accented English in America.

But then a rumor arose that one of my classmates—Jimmy was his English name—had a crush on me. Communication between crushes meant that Jimmy spoke to his best friend, who then relayed it to a girl in the class, who then relayed it to the person sitting behind me, who then whispered, "He likes you," or "He thinks your eyes are pretty."

Jimmy was taller and darker than most of the other kids in the class. He might have been athletically built, but he was painfully shy. He hardly spoke to me, and when he did, he couldn't make eye contact. I had to lean in to hear him. By the end of the following week, Jimmy and I were conveniently sharing classroom chores in the same area; I would push the desks to align with the strip of tape on the floor, and he would flip the chairs over them. I'd never had a boyfriend, but he grazed my hand and I knew it meant we were as good as going steady.

Rumors got around quickly when I kissed Jimmy on the cheek. The class erupted in gossip and I couldn't be happier—for once we weren't talking about classwork, homework, grades, or families. I could actually be involved in the conversation and it didn't matter if I couldn't tell if I actually liked Jimmy. Two days later, holding a broom he was using to sweep up chalkboard dust, he found me on the balcony of our classroom. With a determined and slightly flushed face, he swept my bangs aside in a single movement and gave me a peck on the forehead. A dustpan knocked against the glass and we turned to find the entire class rooting for us, dirty hands and bright, oily faces pressed against the glass. *Wahh! So cool! So sexy!*

The ruckus got us in trouble with the teacher and then, the next day, with the principal. With my poor grades and lack of interest in studying, she was calling my fake Yie Yie into school.

When he arrived, we sat in the dimly lit office in silence. She made us wait for her to start. She wore a fitted red suit with kitten heels, her hair pulled back from her face in a neat way that made her opinion a fact. A petite, shrewd woman who ran the school like a military camp, she had a lot to say.

"This is not America," she stated. "We're not so . . . *whatever* about things. The kids here don't automatically get to go to high school in this country. They have to work hard to get accepted to the next level and then prepare rigorously for college. It's monumentally important that Jimmy stays focused on his future. He needs to be focused on his studies. I will not have her ruin things for him—he's a good kid."

Yie Yie nodded sorrowfully, his eyes downcast. I was mortified and embarrassed for dragging him into this. She continued, from her observation I was a bad influence on the entire class. A distraction. She couldn't allow such promiscuous behavior in her school. She didn't know what my mother was thinking, but it was probably best I went back to school in America, where my behavior would be more acceptable. She dismissed us briskly and brutally.

I could hardly believe it. They were expelling me for a kiss that wasn't even on the lips? I packed and went back to fake Nai Nai and Yie Yie's apartment complex. There, on the phone, my furious mother cursed the day she had me, shouted so loud I held the receiver far from my ear as she flung every foul curse she knew. Before I could respond, she hung up.

In the next couple of days, she tried desperately to find another school, but it was the middle of the semester and no decent boarding school would accept a student now, especially one without any previous education in China.

"It's not about the money," Yie Yie said on the phone the next day. My mother had offered to pay him more to keep me. He paused and then sighed. "She needs to go to school. She needs to go home to America."

Finally, the day before my fifteenth birthday, my mother relented and bought me a ticket to return home. Going home was what I'd wanted since I arrived, but I couldn't stop the stream of tears running down my face. Jimmy and a bunch of our classmates were able to track down my phone number and address. Along with a care package of handmade cards and photos to remember them by, the class called and all sang "Happy Birthday." It made me smile long enough to stop crying and get on the plane. I couldn't process how I felt about leaving, or how to say goodbye.

No one was there to pick me up at JFK. I got some change for my last fifty dollars, found a pay phone, and called the red-brick house. My mother answered and said they were having dinner and weren't going to pick me up. I shook as I held the dead phone in my hand, from fear, from fury, from knowing it was just the beginning. This was what it was going to mean to be back.

Standing in line for a yellow cab, I thought about my dilemma. I wanted to be back in America, but I didn't want to go home. On the cab line, the sky spilled into a sunset. The closer we got, the more I dreaded my mother's wrath. Soon we were on the Cross Island Parkway. I rolled the window down as far as it would go, stuck my head out. A car honked ahead of us and we came to an abrupt stop. Three honks followed. It made me smile; I had missed the honking.

We pulled up in front of the red-brick house and I rang the bell. Jill opened the door, taller and with longer hair. She had gone through puberty; I could see the outline of a sports bra sagging just a bit in the front. She gave no indication that she was excited to see me, and I felt about the same. I closed the door behind me and waited in the living room. My mother walked in from the kitchen a minute later, still chewing.

"Open your suitcase," she said, without a hello or how-was-your-flight. She left a tall glass of water on the coffee table. She dropped my suitcase sideways, loudly unzipped the sides, and deliberately pulled out all the contents. She put aside the contacts, tank tops, and bell-bottoms I had bought at night markets onto the floor. She lifted up a red leather skirt between two fingers.

"What is this?" she asked.

I said nothing.

"Jill, do you think this is *pretty*?" My half sister kept her eyes on my mother and shook her head. My mother laughed, her eyes glassy and mocking. "It's disgusting, right?"

"If you want to sleep in this house, you'll have to throw this out." She nodded toward the high pile with the skirt. She walked toward the stairs and then paused only long enough to say, "Come on, Jill."

I carried the discarded clothes to the trash can outside. It was a shame to throw away the freedom I gained in the last six months. It was the first real taste I had of dressing myself. They were filled with memories of my classmates, my fake grandparents, and Xi'an. Fond memories now. The moon rolled out from under a sheet of clouds and I stood looking up, savoring the familiar breeze. It smelled of freshly cut grass and trash, of home.

I returned to a family who were closer to one another and more distant from me. I was no longer an outsider, but an intruder. My stepfather had not spoken to me since that night in my room, and it seemed that Henry and Jill had also decided to stop speaking to me. My mother's hostility was newly motivated and her fury ran so deep, every word dripped with resentment and venom. I was a child forced on her. In hindsight, the natural next step was to put me to work at the factory. So just like that, my life changed once more.

5

I began moving objects randomly around the house: a book on the table, a toy abandoned on the floor, a sock in the bathroom, one of my siblings' book bags resting against the wall in the hall. I tore leaves off the jade plants sitting in the corner of the dining room, left cabinet doors open, wrote my name in the frosted glass of the bathroom after my showers, and watched the letters drip and then fade. I listened for the sound of slamming doors, steps, and movements in the house. The more isolated I became, the louder I grew. I cleared my throat. My footsteps against the wood floors came down like thunder, the heels of my jeans dragged against the pavement and sidewalks as a companion.

Soon it became a tic, a strange sort of comfort that let me exist out of isolation. I wanted to take up space, make enough sounds, push on the boundaries of the only freedom I had left. I never broke things, but I moved them for the sake of seeing my hand reach out and change something in front of me. I unfolded my stepfather's Taiwanese newspaper, moved my sister's matching hairpins, and bit into the plastic white rice paddle. I liked the sensation of biting down hard, of imprinting my teeth marks on something solid. I bit chopsticks, forks, and sometimes I left bite marks on my own forearm, the taste of soft, salty flesh giving away to piercing pain. It woke me, made me aware of my existence, if only for a minute.

—

On my first day of work at the factory, I showed up to her office. When my mother looked up from her chair, it was as if she couldn't place where she knew me from. There were two seconds of delay before she jumped up.

"Zao chu, zao chu," she said harshly. *Get out, get out.* "Workers are not allowed in here." I tightened my grip on my book bag as she shooed me out.

I watched as a long piece of discarded fabric stuck to my mother's right heel. She was overdressed and out of place in stilettos. I saw her dress most mornings—blow out her hair to a stiff bob, meticulously apply makeup, layer on clothing, and slip on heels—but I'd never seen her at work all dressed up. Everyone else was in knockoff shirts, old jeans, and flats or sneakers, and she came across as oblivious or trying too hard. Here among the machinery and maddening racket, she stuck out. It was embarrassing. She picked up her foot and balanced on a three-inch heel, and then stepped over the piece of fabric.

"Kalei!" she rushed me. She stopped in front of the cutting girls. The women quieted as we approached, and a few of them made room for us. They all wore the same hairstyle, a tight gelled-back ponytail that caught the light whenever their heads dipped. The table was so worn and thick with grime, it was hard to tell what color it had been originally. I patted my palm on the surface and it left an oily residue.

My mother reached over and grabbed a bundle of tan fabric from a large pile in the middle of the table. A ripped strand of nude fabric held fifty or more pieces together. She flattened the material so it sat like a neat stack of paper. It revealed a strange shape resembling the state of Texas. She picked up a pair of yellow trimming clippers and cut the loose strings from two corners. She flipped over to the next piece and snipped the thread from the same corners.

"Are you watching? This is what you do."

"What is it?" I shouted. Thread or lint caught in my nostrils and mouth as I spoke. I rubbed my nose and suddenly understood why some of the workers wore surgical masks. I could barely get a breath of unpolluted air and the dust aggravated my face. I no longer felt clean.

"Sleeves."

"Huh?" I asked, taking baby breaths in and out.

"They go back and the rest of the shirt gets sewed on down there. Sleeves!" She nodded toward the sewing station down the stairs. She shoved the stack into my hand. I imitated my mother's actions and started snipping at the loose ends.

"Then what?" The edges of the plastic scissors dug into my fingers.

"When it's done, you do another stack. Do that until it's all done!" She gestured toward the mountain of fabric in the middle of the table. "Don't lean on the table. Ai yo ah! You start leaning, everyone else will lean too."

I looked down at where she was pointing with the sharp end of the clippers. I was slouching and my stomach was leaning against the edge of the table. Around me, none of the other women were leaning or even slouching. They all stood a few inches from the table. Leaning seemed like a small comfort in all the chaos, and an unnecessarily inhumane prohibition, and I opened my mouth to say so.

A wireless phone on the table rang. I hadn't seen her carrying it, but she must have had it the whole time. She picked up and turned to go.

"Wait," I called after her. "Mommy!"

She stopped at the bottom of the stairs, spinning back around on her heel with slits as eyes.

"What?" she hissed. In Mandarin, she asked the person on the phone to wait. "I told you not to call me that here."

I looked back at the table of women who were pretending not to watch our interaction and felt my face burn. There were countless occasions she lied about who I was, but it was moments like this that I felt most needy. I felt her shaking me off, leaving me the way she had left me with my grandparents in China, and it made me want to hold on tighter. "I—I mean Auntie. Do I come home with you later?"

"No, you leave when everyone else leaves. You're not special, take the train."

I hated her then, her meanness. My face felt flushed as I headed back to the table of women. I hated her almost as much as I hated my dependence on her. I hated that I couldn't help asking, that I wanted to go home with her after all the ways she tried to shake me off. Avoiding eye contact, I took my place among the women.

The prolonged isolated and long hours at the factory ate away any lingering rebellion in me. I could not account for the days, the weeks, or the months. I grew complacent in my unhappiness. At best, there were fuzzy major moments teased out by places and events. And to reconnect to the lost memories would be like holding a mouthful of rice on my tongue, eventually disintegrating into nothing. I was there, but not there. I remember too much and not enough.

—

After missing months of school, Junior High School 194 allowed me to pass seventh grade, but they couldn't put me in the same-ranking class. Instead, they put me in a low-ranked eighth-grade class. I didn't recognize anyone, and all my classes progressed more slowly, with more interruption and less participation. Most of my unfamiliar classmates were more troubled and less interested in learning. A few of the kids picked on me for sitting in the front row and raising my hand. In short, I hated it. I had dreamed of coming back to school, but the reality was a knot in my throat I bitterly swallowed.

Luckily, I had the same lunch period as Grace. We had met in seventh grade and our dysfunctional families kept us uniquely sympathetic to each other. In our time apart, she had grown more introverted.

"You should talk to the guidance counselor," she said one day. I had been complaining about working at the factory for three months by then. Her coarse chin-length hair was always pulled back from her round face. Her eyes were narrow slits, her lips the shape of a Sour Patch peach slice. She carried ChapStick around with her and was always reapplying a moist layer of protection. "Tell them what's happening at home."

"You should be talking," I responded, nodding toward the Korean girls on the other side of the cafeteria. She had her own set of problems she was hiding from. She shifted in her seat, making sure she was out of their line of vision. Sometimes she used my head to block their view.

"They can't help me," she said firmly, her eyes focused on something far away. She took a bite of her ham sandwich that was more of a tear. She was referring to the bullying. I wondered if she had already tried speaking to the guidance counselor. She didn't always tell me everything.

"What would the counselor be able to do anyway?" I asked instead.

She shrugged and looked at the clock, her attention divided. She was waiting for the bell to ring so she could sprint out the double doors. If she waited around, the three girls grabbed at her, stepped on the back of her JNCOs, and pulled her ponytail. They called her names in Korean so no one else could understand. It felt cruel to ask for a translation, so I no longer knew what they said.

Grace wordlessly handed the remainder of her sandwich to me and put on her cross-body Manhattan bag. ChapStick went on her lips and then she was gone. Things were different with Grace since my return; she had learned to adapt and survive without me. I didn't know how to get our friendship back to what it was before I left or how to assure her I wouldn't leave again. I finished the rest of Grace's sandwich and walked down the first floor, even though my next class was on the third floor. The hall was abnormally still between periods. There was a door with an etched nameplate that said GUIDANCE COUNSELOR. A smell of vinaigrette seeped out of the room. A woman with frizzy hair sat behind the desk facing the door. I put my head down and walked quickly by.

—

After returning from China, I picked up where I left off and devoured the two small aisles of romance novels at our local library. Then I expanded my search to the main branch in Flushing. I borrowed as many books as I felt comfortable hiding from my mother. She thought they were inappropriate and would rip them up if she found them. Quickly consuming every title by Elizabeth Lowell, Johanna Lindsey, and Amanda Quick. I didn't need to fight Henry for the remote, try to insert myself into a family that didn't want me, I had something else going on in my life. I needed to find out what Sloan Fairchild was going to say to Carter Madison once they met again, which was bound to happen when they stayed in the same bed-and-breakfast. I was not alone as long as I had a book in my hand, as long as I had the excitement of what awaited me in those pages.

After my return, I found that my family would take vacations without me. I would arrive home to find them gone, unsure of when they'd return. When they came back days later, tanned and with souvenirs from their Carnival cruise, I stayed in my books and out of their way. My mother had no sympathy or pity left for me, and the factory was where she felt I belonged. Since I wasn't ready for the truth yet, I kept watching, reading, waiting for her to come around. She was my mother and I was her daughter, and those were not things that could be changed.

I became exceptionally adept at reading and walking at the same time. The books were an invisible cape, like the protection of the goddess of compassion, Guan Yin. I could survive the cold house, the hours at the factory, the new arrangement at school. It was an escape from the lonely meals, the meanness, and reality.

———

One Saturday, my mother came out of her office and walked over to an empty chair in front of a sewing machine. There wasn't anyone in the section. She'd let them have the day off while she mocked up a new project. She took a seat at the station closest to the office. Her three-inch heels pumped the pedal and her back bent the way all the other sewers did, her body easily remembering the posture. It was a strange moment of past and present. The overhead light washed out the fiery red of her hair to a frizzy glow, and the buzz of the sewing machine moved as one with her hunched body. She straightened only once, to shift the finished fabric and cut the thread. She lifted the piece, and the fabric had turned into a cardigan. She held it up to the light for inspection, turning it over in her hands. I couldn't decide what my mother looked like then: an immigrant, the wife of the boss, or an ambitious businesswoman. Whoever she was, she was exactly where she belonged.

When she was done examining her work against the sample, she gave it to Wang Xian Shen, Mr. Wang. He was the man that handed me my pay. We were paid in cash, in tiny manila envelopes with a receipt stapled to the top that showed rate, time, and total. Loose change rattled whenever he handed over the envelope. I associated him with the sound of coins. The money envelope went straight to my mother when I got home. Mr. Wang bent forward in a deep respectful bow and took the cardigan from her with both hands, as if handling a small child. She turned the light off, stood up, and walked into the office without glancing back. On Monday, I arrived after school to find all the sewing staff in their seats, making hundreds of cardigans from my mother's sample. The entire factory had received its next order.

Here's what I knew even back then: sweatshops and assembly work were an essential part of what it meant to be American in our family. It was the reason my mother was able to build a life with her new husband. It was the reason we could live in a middle-class neighborhood in Whitestone, Queens. It was why we were zoned to good public schools and I was getting a proper education. It was the reason we lived more sheltered lives than our extended family, and had a maid to help with cooking, cleaning, and child-rearing. It was why I knew about American Girl books and felt assimilated enough to claim that I was American.

My parents were the first to purchase a house, and my uncles and aunts followed in their footsteps. The Chinese community seemed to have the same dream: a home, a business, and class mobility in a single generation. Who knew that the great American dream was an assembly line? Our family was an example to so many others, and yet our home was not a happy one.

Much later in life, I am able to understand some of the choices my parents made even if I would have made them differently. It was their job to teach us where we came from, and as much as they felt the tug of our culture, the need to set us up for success always won out. They wanted to protect us from becoming too American, but it was only in shedding one's skin, abandoning China for America, that we could be successful. Even from my limited teenage vantage point, I understood that with my education and future, the factory was a place I was only visiting. I knew that there were things my mother, no matter how mean, could not take away from me. My ability to speak English, my education, a green card, and, later, my citizenship. The question wasn't whether I would leave, but when.

My mother sent me to work to experience the hardship she went through when she first arrived. She wanted me to see how lucky I was compared to other Chinese immigrants. To her point, I was in awe of the cutting girls, their ability to come in every day to a filthy, claustrophobic warehouse and stand ten to twelve hours doing the same menial task a thousand times. I watched their ability to endure and tolerate their dead-end jobs. I knew I would eventually be free of her rules, her scarlet shame, free of the red-brick house and the factory, but for the people I worked with, that was not a certainty. They might never be free of my mother, or at least of this type of factory life. There would likely be a similar job waiting for them anywhere else. Yet they worked, free of bitterness at how America was treating them, or at least that's how it felt in my interactions with them. Their resilience gave me a different perspective to ponder.

In my parents' factory, no one thought about history or lineage. My mother wanted me to experience the hardships of working at the factory so I would listen, be more obedient, be more filial. Instead I saw that she had made it to the top, standing next to my stepfather. She didn't celebrate it, she only thought of keeping her position from then on. She thought about profit. She never considered making conditions better or pay fairer. We aren't those types of people, she would say. We were cogs in a wheel, anything more was beyond our control. Choice does not belong to us. But I thought she could have done more. As a boss, she had made a choice, and I was witness to it.

———

It was the sound of the garage door opening that finally convinced me to talk to someone. The mechanical sound filling the house told me my parents were home. Each night, I braced myself. They expected their kids to greet them at the door, but the thought of her presence, her disdain, her quick temper terrified me. I wanted to run, to hide, to do anything but stand defenseless as danger approached. I realized that my mother's arrival home would always be this way for me. That even if I could make my way to greet them at the door, as I had thousands of times before, this was a feeling I went through every day. I was an animal, trained to react to the sound of the door, trained to be afraid.

Each year of cruelty built upon itself. She didn't speak to me unless it was to tell me to get out of her sight, or a cutting criticism about my hair, my weight, my face, my loudness. Henry and Jill had already learned to keep their distance and to keep secrets from me, but now they were learning something new. My mother was the ringleader, a bully, and the rest of the family followed her example.

—

The door to Mrs. V.'s office was partially open, but I knocked anyway. Her desk sat in the middle of the room, and her glasses reflected the blue of her computer screen as she looked up. She laced her fingers together and leaned in toward me, a gesture I would come to know her by.

I was on my own—had been since I arrived in New York when I was seven years old—and if I wanted out of working at the factory, out of the way my mother treated me, I was going to have to find a way out on my own. No matter how much I endured or how long I worked, it was not going to change the way she treated me. That acceptance let me out of my hopelessness and, in a sense, led me here.

"Can I help you?" she asked, her voice just above a whisper.

She must have been in her thirties or early forties, but at the time, she seemed ancient. She gestured at one of the two seats in front of her desk.

"I don't know," I said, unsure of how to start.

"Why don't you take a seat?"

I sat down, held my backpack close to my chest, using it as a protective layer between me and what I was about to do. There were small trinkets on her desk, and I felt a sudden urge to hold them, to move them around. We had cabinets of things on display at home: expensive bottles of alcohol that business partners gifted to my parents, my stepfather's random coin collection, baby photos of Henry and Jill. None of me. It was my job to dust them sometimes. Dusting was my least favorite chore, it was one of those things that didn't *do* anything, and the cabinet always got dusty again in a few days. What a stupid and useless task.

Before I realized it, I was talking about all the chores my mother made me do, and how much she favored Henry and Jill. She only had enough kindness for them. Every day I just watched them from a quiet place inside myself. I looked away from the small glass object on Mrs. V.'s desk, resisting the sudden urge to touch it.

When the bell rang, she said she would write me a pass for being late, so I could keep talking. It was exhilarating to say things out loud; my suffering had a voice. It felt strangely good to have someone listen openly. She was not telling me I was wrong or that I should be grateful for what I had. My feelings could matter. Sitting before her, my face grew raw with tears.

Mrs. V. had a Queens accent and little to no understanding of what it meant to be Chinese and grow up Chinese American. She was ignorant to what my parents had to overcome and the kind of pressure I felt—the intricacies of assimilating into school and the disparity between the two cultures—but I didn't care about any of that. I didn't mind explaining as long as she fed me her outrage and sympathy, as long as she made me feel seen and heard. The kinder she was, the harder I cried, and the more I opened up. Over the next few weeks, during lunch hour, each story I told her was a weight lifted off me. I told her about how they hid snacks from me, left messes for me to clean up, went on trips and vacations, leaving me for days without so much as a goodbye. I told her about the family cruise.

"How do you know it was a cruise?"

"There's stuff everywhere!" I sobbed. They had brought back souvenirs from the Carnival cruise: T-shirts, plastic cups with the Carnival logo, and key chains. A large photo of them appeared on my mother's nightstand.

Mrs. V. often waited as I took time to explain, handing me a tissue or telling me to take a breath. As each of my mother's secrets came to light, I grew taller and more justified. I sat in her office with a box of tissues on my lap, my book bag forgotten on the floor. A month passed and then another, and something strange began to happen: I reached a kind of plateau. Her surprised expression wore into a troubled frown on her temple, from skepticism to concern. In response to my anguished questions, she told me one day, "Unfortunately, there's nothing we can do to make them be nicer." She let the words linger and interlaced her manicured fingers together. "There's no law for that, but what I can do is make an anonymous call on your behalf to child services. The child labor laws make it illegal for you to be working in a factory for more than twenty hours a week. You're working forty hours? Fifty?"

A knot caught in my throat and an ache tightened along my jawline. I couldn't believe what she was suggesting. "Yes, but it's not about the hours! It's not about the work."

"I know." She gestured with her palm outward. "But the state can't make your mom be nicer to you. No one can make her treat you a certain way. This is how the state can help, if you let it."

Her world seemed impossibly far to me. I thought about how much she didn't understand about where my mother and I came from. Even though we were both living in Queens, we were from different worlds. It felt like she and her perfect nails did not have the capacity to understand what I was telling her. She listened, but many things remained impossible, just as my mother said they did. A silence stretched between us.

"I can't do that. She'll kill me," I finally said.

I felt exposed, like things were out of control. I was wrong for coming here. She could never understand what it was like to be a child of someone who hated you for looking like your father, who felt you were the reason they were unhappy, who felt they could not get rid of you. What would my mother do to me if she found out? The question left too many horrifying outcomes to imagine. I was going to get in trouble and nothing was going to change. I wrapped my arms around my book bag, squeezed the foam shoulder straps, ready to run out if I needed to.

"I do understand, Anna. I don't want to put you in any danger."

"I'm not in *danger*. They're just so . . . . mean." I put on my bag and stood up. "I just want them to be nice to me or . . . or leave me alone."

I could feel my words contradicting one another, the familiar rising frustration.

She leaned back and took a different approach. "I don't think it's going to get better unless we do something about it. And I don't see any other way to make life at home better for you."

The bell rang. It was later than usual, but I made no movements.

"Your mother is treating you horribly, but none of that is illegal. If you let me call, there will be an investigation and you won't have to work in the factory anymore." She leaned both her elbows on the maroon table and put her hands in front of her lips as if she were praying. "Isn't that what you want?"

I couldn't breathe. What I wanted? What I wanted was impossible! I wanted a father who was alive, a mother who cared for and loved me unconditionally. I wanted a relationship with Henry and Jill, with my aunts, uncles, cousins. I knew Mrs. V. was trying to help me, but her words felt like a punch in the gut. How could I call the government on the only family I had ever known? There didn't seem to be enough air. I stood up.

"Just take some time and think about it."

"Okay. But you won't do anything?"

"No, I won't call until it's okay with you."

She was forever patient with me and I was being rude. I bit back an apology, unable to explain the distance I felt. I was sorry, but for what? None of what was happening seemed fair. Usually I left lighter, but today I felt like I needed to wash my face.

The next day, I went back to Mrs. V. I kept talking, trying to find another way, but the more I shared, the clearer it became that there was only one choice and we were both waiting for me to make it. The room filled with silence. She was waiting for me; I didn't know what I was waiting for. Behind her was a view of the street, tree-lined homes with cars parked on either side. I listened for the cars to pass by. When one did, the lighting behind her changed, and I could see her clearly. I waited for those glimpses, hoping for a sign.

I tried going back to my lunches with Grace, pretending things were the way they were before I started seeing Mrs. V. Grace raised her eyebrow when she found me waiting for her at our usual lunch spot. I hadn't seen her in weeks. To her credit, she never asked me about my conversations, just listened if I offered.

We got in line for sandwiches and she gave me her packs of mayo. I liked mayonnaise oozing out the sides of the dry ham sandwich they served. We continued talking as if nothing had happened and she told me about her sister who was a rising singer at their church, about the new H.O.T. album she'd picked up and downloaded to her MP3 player. We sat with our heads tilted toward each other, sharing her earbuds. I couldn't understand any of the lyrics, but it was comforting just to be there.

A week later, I went back to Mrs. V.'s office. I sat in my usual chair. When I opened my mouth, it felt like I was complaining about a problem for which she had already given me a solution. If I continued coming to her office every day, what would it change? I had a way out, and if I didn't take it, wouldn't that mean every wound was self-inflicted?

As we approached the end of the period, I found my right leg twitching. Time was running out. If I was brave enough, strong enough to trust the system, I could help myself. If I kept quiet, my life would remain exactly the same. Those were my choices. "You can call," I said.

"I'm sorry?" There was a pause, as if she was trying to read between the lines. "Call who? Child services?"

"Yes."

"Are you sure?"

I nodded.

"I need you to say it," she said. "You understand once I make the call, it'll be out of my hands. The call will be on the record, they'll take over, and there's no way to unfile it."

I looked at her and then I looked out at the sunny day. I could hear a car approaching, see the glare of the windshield. Otherwise, it was silent. I wanted a sign, but there was only me and what I wanted. "Yes, I'm sure. I want you to call child services."

Fire in Water

6

There was no sense of relief after my conversation with Mrs. V., only dread in the pit of my stomach. I was thirsty, as if my body were running a marathon. I couldn't drink enough water. I lost my appetite, but that was inconspicuous enough. My mother, always conscious of my figure, did not allow breakfast, I ate lunch at school, and dinner was usually a small side plate and some white rice alone.

Mrs. V. had told me to go home and pretend nothing had happened. I was to "act normal." Time moved excruciatingly slowly. I was grateful for the work at the factory. I hid under the sound of the cutting girls' chatter, feeling safer in those moments than in times left to myself. Maybe working at a sweatshop wasn't so bad. It was predictable and that felt safe. I could get used to it, I told myself, the way everyone else had.

I was most self-aware and paranoid at home. I didn't hear Henry's taunts or feel Jill's cold shoulder. I didn't covet what they had. I didn't talk back to my mom. Every small noise made me jumpy, every phrase from my mother's lips had a double meaning. I couldn't focus on anything for long.

At night, I couldn't sleep. I'd played the same scenarios in my head. I was ready for a wide range of possibilities: a quiet phone call, a stranger's knock at the door, cops with handcuffs, sirens and ambulances, multiple scenarios that ended in my death. I was sure she would end my life, but if she didn't, I made a packing list in my head: colored pencils, books I'd borrowed from the library, a photo Grace gave me of the both of us, a graffiti drawing a classmate had done of my name, my journal, and one set of clothing. I would leave everything else. Packing a bag was too risky, so I repeated the list in my head. I went over where they were. The colored pencils were in my desk. The photo on a shelf. The journal hidden behind my bed. The sketch already in my book bag.

By the end of the second day, I began entertaining the possibility that nothing was going to happen at all. Maybe Mrs. V. had forgotten. Or they hadn't believed her. The Office of Child and Family Services was too busy. It had all been a mistake and it was all for the best.

That night, my mother's cordless phone slammed on the kitchen table. My fingers paused over the porcelain bowl in the sink. The regal blue patterns on the matching set mimicked an old Chinese dynasty crest, but we had bought them from Jin San, a Chinese grocery store my mother frequented. It had everything from on-site butchers, fresh seafood in tanks, fruit and vegetables, to rice cookers and kitchen utensils, herbal medicine, and over-priced ginseng behind a special counter.

"Man ju fu you zao qie de," my mother said over the running faucet. *You don't have to go to the factory tomorrow.*

It's happening, I thought. I felt light, as if I were leaving the conversation, rising out from my body and hovering over the long narrow kitchen.

"Well, that was my brother," my mother said, switching to Mandarin to speak to my stepfather. There was lead in her voice. "They're being audited too. And there's a fine."

I stood perfectly still. My mother never had conversations in front of me; she believed adults knew things adults knew, and children knew what parents told them. If she was having a serious conversation with my stepfather at the kitchen table, it meant she wanted me to know what I had done.

"They are coming here. To our *house*."

"We don't have anything to be afraid of. We've talked about this already," he responded calmly.

I knew, without turning around, that my stepfather was sitting at the dining room table reading *The Taiwan Times*, his nightly ritual. On the bridge of his nose perched a pair of gold-framed '80s glasses reflecting the overhead lights. A bottle of Heineken, which he sipped periodically, sweated on the glass table. He liked his alcohol, but my mother, with her measuring eyes and firmly set lips, allowed him only two drinks a night.

"Duai! We've done nothing wrong. They can't take our kids away." A tremor passed through my mother's voice and cut right through to my body.

"*My* kids!" She slammed her palm on the mahogany table and I felt my baby hairs jump up on my forearm.

My kids. She was talking about Henry and Jill, of course. They were her kids and I was just a drain on her resources, a problem rather than a person. I focused on rinsing out the bowl and finishing the dishes. My hands were just like hers—wide-palmed and thick-knuckled with spider-long fingers.

I had waited precisely three days for this: the shit to hit the fan, the walls to cave in, my life to change forever. My mind prepped me for a raging mother: acidic words, feigned health issues, broken bones, and blood. What was it going to be?

The water was hot and my hands were turning pink and pruney. After years of practice, her words scrubbed off like oil in soapy water. I had done the right thing. It was my mantra as I rinsed the lather off. As far as I was concerned, if calling the Office of Child and Family Services could get me out of working in the factory, and out of my mother's angry path, the end justified the means.

"Hao la, hao la," my stepfather said in Mandarin. *Enough.*

"Everything is under our name, so if we get in trouble, they will too," she continued. I hadn't thought about the repercussions, I'd only worried about what my mother would do once she found out what I'd done. For the first time since the call was made, I thought about other people—Henry, Jill, my aunts and uncles, the people at the factory. They had done nothing wrong and didn't deserve this. I scrubbed a pair of chopsticks, shook myself free of the guilt, and stared at the sponge gripped under my fingernails.

"This is what you wanted, is it?"

She threw a string of curses. *Cunt! Go die somewhere far from here. No daughter of mine. Cursed to have a child like you. I should die for having a child like you.* The force of her words, her anger—which always threatened violence—made my fingers slip across the wet surface of a bowl as I flipped it over onto the dish rack. What more could she do to me? I was afraid of the answer.

"Lin, how much do you think they've been fined? A thousand dollars? At least, right?"

He grunted, and took the bait. "At least."

"Lian tou duo guan la!" she said in Mandarin. *She's losing all our faces!*

If I pulled the thin lip of the rice bowl with enough force, it could go. The whole slippery bowl could crumble in my hands. There could be a terrifying amount of blood, maybe enough to warrant a hospital visit and enough chaos to make this seem small. Maybe it would be enough to permanently scar my hands, sever any semblance to my mother.

"How long do you think it'll take my brother to make back the money for the fine? They don't earn much at their location."

This time he chose to read on. My stepfather knew her ruse. Only a single rustle was made as he turned the page.

Her bare feet pounded against the kitchen tiles and then she was behind me. I focused on slowly rotating another bowl, running the lather off under the hot water. It took all my effort to keep my hands steady.

Now that we were here, now that I'd forced her hand by doing the very thing that caused her to say the things I feared most, I found I could not speak at all. I could not justify my actions. The

suds on my hands blurred in front of me, scalding water burned
my fingers red. I carefully placed the bowl gently between the
other ones on the dish rack. I had done this, and now I deserved
whatever punishment was coming.

"Are *you* going to pay them back?" She breathed the words
into my hair. Her warm breath and spit tickled my neck. I bit the
inside of my lip and focused on the pain as I squeezed my teeth
together, waiting for the taste of blood.

"Do you have the *money* to pay them back?" she pressed.

The back of my neck prickled and I braced for impact. When
I didn't respond, she spat, "Do you think we're afraid of you?"

There was almost a sense of relief now, knowing the waiting
was finally over. Picking up the last bowl to lather, I admitted I
didn't care if this hurt my mother. I would do anything to get out
of the factory, out of this miserable home. I wanted to hurt her as
much as she hurt me.

"Do you think *I'm* afraid of *you*?"

I was slow to take in her question. Afraid? As the word registered, it sounded unnatural. It didn't sound like a thing mothers
said to their daughters, or even words that belonged together. I
wondered how many mothers in history have asked that question.
Do you think I'm afraid of you? I felt giddy, like I wanted to laugh
and cry at the same time. The ludicrous role reversal made me feel
cheated out of something so *mine*. I couldn't understand how she
had made it hers. How had *she* become the victim?

Her index finger dug into the back of my head as she shoved
hard. My bangs fell into my eyes, and for a moment, I welcomed
the darkness, her violence.

I saw it then, as I turned around, the pure expectation in her eyes. It was a familiar look, a look that told me to comply. There was no reasoning, no bargaining, no talking. It did not require explanation. She had told me a hundred times what she expected from me, but I kept fighting, kept insisting. It was clear now that it was her expectations I had failed. I was raised in an American classroom, taught the privileges and freedoms of a white person's history and culture. I had betrayed her with my Americanness. It didn't involve my half siblings; it had always been about us. And it came down to trust. And a daughter that did not trust her mother was as much of an anomaly as a mother that sacrificed her daughter. In Chinese opera, all love stories end in tragedy and someone always dies. There are no happy endings because duty is more important. As my mother's daughter, it was my duty to serve her, to obey and please her. I was aware of my fundamental flaw. My mother and I were at the cusp of being who we would always be to each other and there would be no happy ending for us.

I used a wet hand to push my bangs out of my eyes. Her face was inches from mine, close enough for me to smell the souring vinegar on her breath. As quickly as the thought of our shared struggle, our difference came to me, it was gone. Next to the sink, the dish rack was full of small porcelain bowls. I was usually still hungry after a bowl of rice, but I wasn't allowed to eat more. There was no room for my hunger in this family. "No," I finally forced out. I'd found my anger. Our eyes met, hard and unmoving. "I know you're not afraid."

She cackled, delighted that I was finally responding. "Do you think we care about you now?" Her eyes were shards of broken glass people warn you to walk around. Invisible, dangerous glass that hides well in all kinds of lighting. "*No one* cares about you."

"I know"—I was out of breath, trying to form the words that I needed to share with her; words that I had been waiting for the better part of my life to articulate—"you don't care."

The words left a dryness in my mouth. I wanted them to be true so that I could no longer feel, so that I could finally sever ties between us and accept who I was. I wanted my words to be daggers, the way her words always wounded me. There would be no loss, only relief. Now I was never going to be accepted in the family. I was finally rejecting them.

"All right, all right," my stepfather said. He turned another page. It was the only sound in the room besides our breathing. He liked being the peacemaker, and for a long time, I thought he was the only person that could calm my mother. Her savior and mine, I had thought, but after he and my mother sent me to China, I knew better.

Her shoulders slumped forward as she turned and walked back to the spotless kitchen table. The half-mooned night washed across her seat as she sat down again. She tugged on the collar of her pink quilted robe, as if cold. Her face was clean and fresh from her bath. The gentle sun spots high on her cheekbones were visible and they made her look vulnerable. "Let's go up, I'm tired."

"Okay, okay," he said, finishing up his last article.

She stared as if trying to make out invisible writing on the cabinets covering the kitchen wall. For a second, she looked thoughtful and innocuous. There was a rhythm to her madness, a snarling and thrashing cruelty that calmed once spent. Her hand came to her gaunt chin as if she'd just remembered something. I could see what was coming next. She was receding against the magnitude of my actions.

"No child of mine could betray me like this, right? It's impossible," she mumbled, almost to herself.

He grunted and shrugged in his good-natured way. She stood up first. They would pick up their kids on the way up to the master bedroom and spend the rest of the evening watching a movie or Taiwanese sitcom as a family.

"You wouldn't do that. Right, Ah Na?" she asked, looking back at me.

"Right," I lied, a ghostlike whisper before I could stop myself. Over time, I found out it was easier not to antagonize her. My stepfather stood, took off his wire-rimmed glasses, and laid them over the traditional Chinese text. He drained his empty beer one more time. They were almost the same height as they left together.

One by one, I removed all the chairs surrounding the kitchen table, swept, and then mopped the floor on my hands and knees, just the way my mother liked. The whole kitchen smelled of Murphy's Oil by the time I was done.

I wiped the sweat from my forehead, leaving a trail of hot water in its place. I could smell the oil from the sponge on my fingers. Only a pair of chopsticks was left in the sink. Ridged teeth marks, indented from years of use, had worn into the smooth wood. The dishes were done, and for the first time since the beginning of the conversation, I felt safe.

—

A week after I stopped working at the factory, a bilingual social worker arrived at our house. Her name was Mary and she gave us the option of seeing her together or separately. My mother and I each chose to see her alone.

Mary didn't take sides and liked to remain neutral. She came and sat with me in our living room, on the end of the leather couch that I always waxed extra to get it to shine like the rest of the cushions. I didn't find her sympathetic like Mrs. V., she didn't seem to care all that much about how awful things were, how I was feeling or how I was dealing with all the change. We only talked about achieving goals. She talked to me about volunteering and how I could find a part-time job through the school now that I was not working at the factory. Local businesses often posted on job boards in high schools. Did I know where to go to find that information at my high school? Following her advice, I went for an interview and walked out of a dentist's office with my first real part-time job.

Mary was able to convince my mother it would be a good thing to let me out of the house, and earn my own way. She talked her into letting me keep the money I earned as a dental assistant and see friends when I wasn't working. Up until then, I was never allowed out with friends or to keep the money I earned. Other changes were immediately noticeable, too. My mother was still cold and angry, but she no longer criticized me every time she saw me. She stopped commenting on my weight, my face, my hair, my posture, my clothes, my existence. She no longer saw a child she could remold or a child that was sent to punish her. Now, with Mary's help, I was just a person that she needed to put up with for a while longer. What I truly wanted—to be a part of the new family my mother had created—was impossible, but fixing our family was not Mary's goal, less conflict was.

A month after I started working at the dentist's office, Mary convinced my mother to take me to open a bank account. I met her in front of the Q16 terminus in Flushing. She got out of a black Jin Ma, and I followed the echoes of her heels down the sidewalk, past McDonald's to the Queens County Savings Bank.

Flushing was always bustling with commuters, peddlers, and trinket sellers on street corners. She didn't look around or make eye contact with anyone, there was just the focus on her destination. As usual, she weaved quickly through the crowd, and I half-ran to keep up with her.

Creating an account at our local community bank took less than ten minutes. I spoke to the teller in clear English and my mother passed over her license and my birth certificate. The woman behind the glass gave us a form to fill out and after a few keystrokes, she handed me a bank book with tiny grid lines and even tinier print. I deposited my first two checks from the dentist's office and couldn't believe I was finally able to keep the money I was making. I was dumbfounded and so happy I couldn't stop smiling. My mother had this strange look on her face, as if she didn't understand why the small booklet meant so much. The mutual relief took us by surprise as we walked out. As I waited for the bus home and she called another Jin Ma back to work, we recognized it as the first moment of truce we'd had in a long time.

7

Mary's office in Midtown Manhattan was unexpectedly messy; files were piled up so high they toppled over, an unplugged lamp sat in the middle of the carpeted room, old laptops were stacked in a dark corner. The walls were made of wood panels, and it felt like we were enclosed in the belly of a ship.

She used to come to the house, but she was too busy now. Here, she seemed absentminded, as if waiting for the hour to tick by so she could visit her next family. She barely made eye contact while I described how my parents took my half siblings to see my aunts and uncles but left me home. I lost my place speaking as I followed her gaze to one of her desk piles.

"So, this will be our last session," she said.

It was only the third or fourth time I'd visited her in Manhattan. Mary had changed my relationship with my mother in just a few months. I had a part-time job, a bank account, and freedom to see my friends. My standard of living had risen with Mary's helpful interventions. She tempered my mother's rage, convinced her to wait before reacting, and gave us the distance we needed to soothe our resentments. She stood between us, a mediator.

"What? Why?" I asked. I was gripped with the fear that it would all go back to the way it was before.

"It's time," she said simply.

"What if she's mean to me again?"

"She won't be," she stated flatly.

Mary's terse, abrupt manner reminded me of all my Chinese relatives, but she spoke English fluently. She was the first glimpse of my two worlds coexisting, Chinese and American. The life I had at home with my family and the student life I had with my friends were always at odds. In Mary, I saw the benefits of education and upbringing, of being both Chinese and American. There was a future outside of factories, nail salons, dry cleaners, and restaurants, and I could see it plainly.

She had a job with autonomy, and her opinions mattered. Her clients listened and took her advice. More important, my mother listened and took her advice. Just by her example, she taught me there was a way out and that there were no limits to who I could be when I grew up. She was the first Chinese American figure that gave me that sense. I couldn't verbalize it at the time, but she was a role model, an inspiration. Our relationship was standard protocol for her, but her appearance felt extraordinary in my life. Her withdrawal was equally devastating.

"There's not much more I can do," she said dismissively.

Make her love me, I wanted to scream.

Looking back now, I can see why she ended our sessions. As a social worker Mary's workload kept her from continuing to see me. She had made concrete changes for us and I was not in danger. There were other families, files that toppled visibly over her desk, that needed her attention. When she stopped coming by the house, she explained that she needed to move on, but I was too afraid of my reality without her. I nodded, thanked her, and stood up. I had thought that coming to her office would prolong our time together, but it only delayed the inevitable.

8

In 1985, my mother came to the United States with a single borrowed suitcase and two outfits. She shared a small room with other immigrants. She slept on the floor, borrowed clothes, and made her peanut butter sandwiches to stay warm against the cold winter. Like many other immigrants, she came with nothing of value. What she handed down had no material value, either.

Like many of our arguments, we fought over something I wanted. I had just started high school and wanted to take swimming classes. Neither my mother nor I knew how to swim and my mother had an irrational fear of water. I wasn't sure if experience had formed her aquaphobia—if so, I hadn't been told about it—but she was raised to stay away from what she didn't know or understand. I, on the other hand, was growing up American. At home, all I knew were limitations, but at school I was just another kid who wanted to have friends, who wanted to be good at things, and who wanted to learn how to swim. If I didn't know how to swim, here was an opportunity to take lessons. All I had to do was convince my mother and get permission.

The problem was, I had a near-drowning experience when I was five years old and still living with my grandparents in China. I slipped on some green moss collecting at the foot of a well near their house. My cousin, who is four years older and was my playmate that day, watched as the well soundlessly swallowed me. Shock took hold of her, leaving her speechless until she was screaming at the top of her lungs. A neighborhood uncle passing heard the shrieking and came running. I woke up on my grand-parents' bed, with a room full of familiar neighbors who had come to see the child fished out of a well.

My mother was sleeping off a long shift at the garment factory in New York at the time. When word finally got to her days later, her horror felt dramatic over the landline. Time passed differently for the two countries, and her distressed voice, cutting in and out, made the distance more apparent. She asked over and over how it could have happened, still processing the days-old information. No one had answers for her, everyone had done their share of gossiping and processing. I turned away from the voice as I often did, looking outside the kitchen to the front entrance—past my grandfather perched in his usual spot puffing on a cigarette—toward my blue tricycle, at my days without her. She had been gone for years by then, a lifetime for me.

Now she refused to sign the release form or buy me a bathing suit, the two requirements for Beginner Swim. It was as if she were making up for the incident at the well, preventing another occurrence and finally protecting me. My resentment stirred. If no one had told her about the accident, she would have never known. She hadn't been there, so who was she to tell me what to do now? I stifled a response, held on to my anger, the way she often held on to hers.

She argued that we were both fire signs, and fire signs should never tempt fate or, in this case, water. There were certain combinations that should be avoided. Fire and water was one of them. The five elements—fire, earth, water, air, and wood—are meant to be heeded. Wood and air fuels fire, fire forms earth, and earth feeds wood.

"What happens to fire in water?" she asked. "Think about it."

This is stupid, I wanted to say. *I'm a teenage girl, not fire.*

I forged my stepfather's signature and bought a bright violet one-piece bathing suit with money I stole from her purse. Stealing cash from her wallet was a habit I had picked up, justified by all the things she bought my siblings.

I left the evidence hanging from my gym locker, but of course, my mother knew. My hair and skin smelled permanently of chlorine and betrayal. The pool stripped my long hair of oil, tangling it into knots so I had to tie it in a ponytail after each class. It was then, halfway through the semester, that my mother came home sick one day. She woke up from her feverish nap and called me to her side. The powder-pink shades were drawn, her room a dim, rosy-hued cave. I could barely make out her slight figure sitting up in the queen-size bed.

"I saw you in school," she sounded strange and hesitant.

"There was a large pool and the water was black. You were face-down, floating, not moving. Your hair was everywhere."

She looked at me, her eyes glassy and bright against the gaunt pallor of her face. Her tone was somewhere between threatening and pleading. It gave me goose bumps and I was suddenly afraid. I imagined her silhouette at the edge of the school pool, bent over, tugging on a dead body, the flat water shifting and rippling as she frantically fought to move me.

"I tried to get you over to the side, but you were too far. That's when I realized the pool water wasn't black, it was your blood." She paused and then implored, "You've got to stop taking swimming classes. Listen to your mother."

I can't remember if I promised her that I would. But after a dozen classes or so, it was clear I had no talent for swimming and I had developed a fear of my own. My body stiffened whenever I tried to get horizontal in the water, my belly a dense stone gravitating to the bottom of the pool. Arms flailing, breath wild and erratic, I panted in the water. Panic set my brain on fire. I finished the class, but the water never felt natural. The bottom of the blue bed beckoned me, calling for my death in my mother's voice.

9

The night before I left for college, my mother knocked on my bedroom door. She held a tall glass of steaming hot water with the tips of her index finger and thumb. According to Chinese medicine, hot water is good for digestion, and she always drank it as hot as her lips could handle. Steam billowed into her face as she took thimble-sized sips. She never knocked, so I knew something was up.

"You need to tape the bottom of that," she said, pointing to the box. I had saved a single giant box from the dentist's office and carried it all the way home.

She set the water on the desk. We had three sets of the same desk in the kids' rooms; two with pink borders and trimmings, and one with blue.

"It's not that heavy."

"Take it out and do it right," she said. "Listen to me."

"I just put all of the stuff in here." I leaned back and crossed my legs on the carpet. Usually I ignored her suggestions and demands, but she seemed to be in a good mood, and I didn't want my last night to be upsetting. Avoiding each other was the best we could do lately.

"When are you leaving?" she asked as I began removing notebooks from the box.

"Eight in the morning."

"Hozanna is taking you?"

"Rosanna. Rose," I corrected her. "Her mom is taking us."

I tried to keep the rise out of my voice. I would have loved my mother to drive me up to college, but she'd never asked what colleges I had applied to, where I was accepted, or my final decision. Once I started speaking English fluently and passing grades, she lost interest in my education. She didn't care about my report cards—which were always better than Henry's and sometimes better than Jill's—she didn't care about my PTAs, plays, music performances, or graduations. I did the research for college on my own and applied with money I'd saved. Mary was gone, but the independence we'd won remained. She had been right. My mother had let me keep my job at Dr. Krell's. I worked there after school every day and half days on Saturdays. He trained me to take X-rays, to make mouth guards, order dental supplies, speak to insurance companies. After three years, I learned everything from how to be a dentist's assistant to how to manage the front office. I worked all through summer and had just worked my last day.

Tomorrow I was going to college. Fortunately, my friend Rose was going to the same school. She had visited the college and liked it. We were going to be roommates and her mom was giving us a ride.

"We should be there in three hours and then Rose's mom will take us to buy stuff," I told her. I left out that Rose wasn't too pleased about me and my things occupying space in her mother's car.

For a minute, only the sound of Scotch tape filled the room.

"Are you taking everything?"

"I can't fit everything, I only have one suitcase and this box."

"Well, we might be redoing this room. Whatever you leave, we'll toss."

"Where am I supposed to stay when I come back?" I asked.

"Ah Na," she sighed. "You're old enough now. I think it's time, don't you? We're going to turn this room into an office for him."

Him was my stepfather. "I was already married at your age," she said. She picked up her drink carefully and blew. "I just want some peace and quiet. He's not so young anymore and we just want to pass our time peacefully. I think it's time I live my own life now, don't you?"

Her quiet reasoning made it harder to find the anger that would allow me to rise out of my shame. What kinds of conversation were other kids having with their parents tonight? The excitement of starting college was gone, and in its place, a familiar numbness.

"Here, I have something for you."

I could smell the clean scent of Biolage conditioner off her damp hair as she dropped a white envelope in my lap. Without looking, I knew it was cash. I wanted to throw the envelope in her face and tell her to keep her fucking money. I didn't need anything from her.

"And call me when you get there. Let me know you got there safe," she said cheerfully, pausing before she shut the door.

My body refused to budge. The gentle weight of the envelope crushed me. I should have said something, stood up for myself in some way. Told her to keep her money. She had turned my last evening into the night I lost my home. I sat still until my legs fell asleep under me and cramped. Finally, I opened the envelope on my lap, my pride had a price—and when I counted, it was worth two hundred dollars.

10

A few weeks into my first semester at Binghamton University, I received an invoice that said I had yet to complete my college-loan process. I'd paid the deposit using the money I saved working at the dentist's office, but I owed for room and board, tuition, and a mandatory meal plan for first-year students. My stepfather made too much money for me to qualify for any financial aid, and to qualify for federal loans, I needed my parents to cosign. They were waiting for the signature.

The dread set in easily, a familiar guest in my body. Holding the thin paper, I acknowledged the angst I'd had since I arrived. College was too good to be true, I didn't belong here. I wasn't entitled to carefree days of classes and campus life. I didn't deserve to build my own future. Education was a privilege for Henry and Jill, not me. Just as I feared, this new start was out of my reach. Now they would surely find me out for what I was, an imposter.

I waited until midmorning, when I was sure I was alone in my dorm room, and then dialed my mother's number for the first time since my arrival. With how we had left things, I hated that I was calling so soon. I wished I could show her how independent I was, how I didn't need her to survive and live, but here I was, doing the exact opposite. She had kicked me out days ago, and I was calling her for help. My palms grew sweaty with each ring, my shame mounting.

"You didn't call when you got there," she said as soon as she picked up. There was never hello or goodbye with my mother.

"Oh, sorry . . . I need to take out a loan for school."

"Okay," she said, "so take one out. What does it have to do with me?"

I swallowed, my mouth felt dry. How was I going to get her to do this for me? She had washed her hands of me, packed me away, and turned my room into an office.

"I need a signature, from you or Baba. The school says he makes too much money for me to get any financial aid, but I can take out a loan."

"Fukunang," she said flatly. *Impossible.*

"I'm looking for a job now. You won't have to pay for anything, all I need is for you to sign the document. I'll pay them back slowly when I'm done with school." I tried to keep my voice steady and neutral. She hated whining, almost as much as tears.

"They'll kick me out if I don't pay them," I croaked, admitting my worst fear. It was only now that I was away, living outside of the red-brick house, that I could see things with some clarity. My mother's love for me was not as high as a mountain, as vast as the sea, or as big as the sky. It could not endure the trials of the human condition. Her unwillingness to stand up for me or help me had been repeated over and over in my childhood, and now, for the first time in my life, I could admit it. I was far enough from home to accept certain truths, and I could almost forgive her for all of it, if she would help me now.

"I gave you my answer. If you don't have money, why don't you take some time off and work?" she suggested. "Save some money and then go back to school."

I could hear her cold smile as my mind raced. Her solution was unthinkable to me. I didn't know how to start a life where college was not the goal. "No, I have to go to school now."

"Everything always has to happen immediately, just the way you need it to! Wake up! We don't live in that kind of life."

I felt the rising panic in my chest, a dark flowering that rose to my throat. I looked around the dorm room that I shared with Rose and a third roommate. We had a common space, a small living room area, with two other girls from Long Island. How far this life felt with my mother on the phone telling me to wake up. How much I wanted to be like them. Moving in during orientation, I met all their families; fathers who helped carry furniture and put up shelves, mothers who helped pick out bedspreads, toiletries, and warmer clothes for the fall weather. Families met families, went out to meals. I was the only person moving in alone. I told myself that these feelings weren't permanent and that I belonged as much as they did. But she was telling me otherwise.

I wanted to make it so the people around me would not see me as a burden. Starting college was supposed to be the beginning of that—of being the same as everyone else. If I had to leave before I got started, I had already failed. And without college, without this education, how could I make something of myself? How could I achieve a life outside of a sweatshop?

"Is there anything else?" She sighed. "I have work to do."

There were so many tears flowing, I couldn't see. "No, that's it," I said as loudly and clearly as I could.

And just like that, the call was over.

I wiped my face with the back of my hand. I had no one else besides my mother. She had isolated me from my stepfather's family and her family, and I didn't know anyone from my father's family. I had friends, but they were seventeen and eighteen years old. Who could help me? How long would it take before the school kicked me out?

The next morning, I washed my face with cold water, added thick eyeliner to my swollen eyes, and walked down to the financial aid building. The office was in the heart of the campus, but it felt deserted and quiet. The director of financial assistance sat at a desk, one of three, in a spacious room with oversized windows. A few plants competed for sunlight. When he called me in, we sat at the middle desk. I found myself shaking as I explained the situation, my voice cracking. My conversation with my mother flooded back into my mind, and then I couldn't figure out what to do with my hands. How could I appeal to a stranger when I couldn't appeal to my own mother?

The director was a well-spoken, well-dressed middle-aged

guy. He wasn't uncomfortable with my overflow of emotions, and his forehead creased as he leaned in, struggling to understand what I was trying to say. He looked at his computer and asked me to spell my name.

"How old are you?"

"Eighteen—turning nineteen next month."

"If your parents won't cosign your loan . . . let me see. So it doesn't look like you qualify for any other type of financial aid. Unless you claim yourself independent from your family, you will need to get them to cosign. I don't see any other way."

"I *am* independent from them. I've been independent for a long time."

"That'll be the challenge to prove." He paused as he scratched his head. "Our school policy, which is aligned with the state policy, says you have to be twenty-four to claim independence from your parents. The only other way to show proof is to establish a case and file it with the state."

"What kind of proof?" I asked, my stomach a heavy knot of dread. "We can call my mom and you could talk to her yourself."

He paused, turned back around to face me. I had difficulty meeting his eyes. "No, that won't work. It can't be your word or her word."

Someone walked into the office behind me and I grabbed another tissue to hide the makeup running down my face.

"Maybe I could get my guidance counselor from my junior high school or this woman that was our social worker."

"Oh, if your family has been assigned a social worker, a letter from them will do!"

He gave me instructions. I would do whatever it took to stay in school, even though I didn't know how I'd be able to convince Mary to help me.

"It's none of my business but . . ." he said hesitantly, as I stood up. "We have free counselors on campus. I think it would help you to talk about some of this. I can set up a time for you, if you like."

"Will going to the counselor help me stay in school? Help my case? I just want to make sure I can stay in school."

"No. It would be unrelated," he said gently, "but I think it would help you."

I didn't need therapy, I needed a solution. But I was afraid to refuse him. I gave him a long look and nodded. "Okay. I'll see her."

—

It took me a week to reach Mary. We had not spoken in two years.

"Your case is closed, Anna," she told me.

I explained the situation to her. "All I need is for you to say my parents won't support me, and send it to the school. I've already typed up the letter."

There was no answer on the other end of the line.

She cleared her throat and congratulated me on getting into college. Then she told me she was not interested in getting between my mother and me. It was a practiced line I'd heard often when we met.

I swallowed and took a breath and tried again. "She kicked me out and told me I can't come back. And if I can't stay here, I don't know where I'll go or what I'll do. All of my friends are in college. Please, you have to believe me."

I couldn't keep my voice from pleading. This had to work, she needed to help me. It was my last option. "Please, if you don't believe me, you can call her—"

"No, that won't be necessary." She sighed. "I believe you. Give me a few days—"

The days following the call with Mary were both unbearably slow and seemed to pass in a dense fog. I hated waiting. I bounced among worrying that she'd back out, change her mind, forget, or a combination of any of those possibilities. What if she sent the letter and it wasn't enough?

I had too much time on my hands, and no longer saw the point of going to class. On the other hand, if I was going to be kicked out of college, these were the only days I'd be able to spend as a college student. I walked around in a daze, exhausted by the same cycle of doubt. It was painful to be this close to having what I wanted, only to have it taken away.

In the meantime, I went to work at my job at a Japanese hibachi restaurant a few miles off campus, where I wore a blue kimono with orchids and waited tables. I disliked it immediately, but I was grateful to have money coming in. I thought about the cutting girls and wondered if waitressing was where I was going to get stuck. Was that where I would end up working every day? I imagined waiting tables for the next forty, fifty years. I didn't want to know what life would hold if Mary's letter didn't come.

A week later, I barged into the director of financial aid's office with the letter, held high like a blazing torch.

I held my breath as he read it carefully. He nodded as he read, as if he could hear the words. He brightened immediately.

"That's it!"

They were the sweetest two words I'd heard spoken. Relief washed over me and I was sure this was the happiest moment of my life. I couldn't believe it. There was too much air in the room. My chest opened and then so did my face.

He said he'd help me file it and then the financial aid office would process the change. It would be a few weeks, but he could expedite it and let the financial office know now. He left the piece of paper on his desk and stood up to walk me out. I hugged him, embarrassing him to a point where he let out an awkward laugh. He gave me a firm pat on the back and sent me off with his entire box of Kleenex.

As I walked back out into the fall weather, I couldn't believe how crisp the air felt in my lungs. How bright the green grass looked. How young and happy the students seemed. Their laughter was contagious. What a difference twenty minutes made! I could feel the sun on my skin again, taste the salt from my tears. Suddenly, I was ravenous, hungry in a way I hadn't been for days. For food, for books, for class, for my next four years, for life and light. I wondered, if I had never called child services and never met Mary, would I have been able to go to college now? I didn't want to dwell on it, but it was terrible and surprising how things worked out. I was a part of the world again—with so much joy and gratitude, it hurt.

11

During spring break, I stayed with Rose and another childhood friend, Jess. One night we went to a new bar in Flushing. The doorman looked up and stopped me from entering. He stared at my license. I was preparing one of my eye rolls when he started speaking in my native dialect, in Wenzhounese. He called me by my full name, Qu Na, and then followed by dropping the family name and repeating it in the familial way, "Ah Na." Each time he chanted it, I dug deeper until I pulled out who he was—my cousin, my oldest aunt's eldest child.

"Ziqi, Ziqi," he said then, quietly. "Danny."

It hit me. When I was nine, I had a crush on him. He was the only cousin on my mother's side that immigrated before I did. He was the aloof and surly type; ignoring his nagging mom, taking the car out until five in the morning. I was his annoying kid cousin, the tomboy with too many questions. His mom made him be nice to me though: I was fatherless.

It'd been over a decade since I'd laid eyes on him, but there he stood, shorter than I remembered, and too skinny. He was barely thirty but looked older. He worked hard, like my uncles—and just like them, he was handsome. He handed my license back to me, and I moved awkwardly to the side as he continued to ID the line of people behind me. I didn't know where to start. I asked what he was doing there.

"I own the place." He squinted and gave me a side-eye. "Didn't your mother tell you?"

"No, not really," I responded, not sure about how much he knew. I hadn't been home since I left for college that awful night. "We don't talk much."

Our mothers were close, though my mother had a habit of not talking about unpleasant topics such as my dead father and me. The last time I saw my aunt, she was sorting through plastic bins of toys in their basement. It was her job to ready the van in the mornings before her husband and son went to sell them on the street.

My mother thought it was too close to panhandling, but seven days a week my uncle and cousin set up a table in Flushing with a twin-size sheet thrown over it. They sold key chains, bobbleheads, Transformers, anime and cartoon action figures, cell phone trinkets and cases. All were bought for nickels and dimes, and sold for dollars. While they were out during the day, my aunt sat on a cushion, bent over a sewing machine in the den she'd converted. She hoped when they bought the house in Queens that the sweatshop work was behind her—they had their American dream, the house, the front lawn, the two kids—but then the reality of their mortgage hit. Bundles of fabric were dropped off in the morning and the sewing machine could be heard vibrating late into the night.

"How long have you been here?"

He shrugged. "We may sell."

"Oh, business not good?"

My Wenzhounese came out tongue-tied, the order of the words wrong and hesitant. I had trouble understanding him, too. He grew annoyed after I asked him to repeat himself for the third time. I couldn't remember the last time I spoke to anyone besides my mother in Wenzhounese and it was difficult to hear the sharp changes in his words. He asked if English was easier and I nodded. But his English was almost as awkward and slow as my Chinese. His accent was so thick I had to lean in and pause before responding. I felt slightly embarrassed for the both of us. We were family, but we'd lost our common language—or I'd lost it—and there was no familiar tongue to go back to.

There was a time when I would have gone anywhere with him. Once, a few years after I arrived in the United States, he said he'd take me fishing on the East River. I didn't question the sudden burst of generosity and quickly asked my mother if I could go.

Fishing! I had never been. Even my stepdad didn't take his kids fishing. The week passed excruciatingly slowly and I'd never tried so hard to be on my best behavior. Suddenly, I didn't care that my half siblings got the meat of the fish and I got the tail, that their clothes were store-bought and mine were leftover samples from the factory, or that I was given chores while they watched cartoons all day—I was going fishing! That morning in bed, I was afraid to open my eyes. Would the sky be dark and heavy with rain? Would he change his mind or worse, forget? I squeezed my eyes shut and said a prayer, *please, please, please.* He showed in the late afternoon hours. An impatient honk announced his arrival. I ran out and the screen door slammed as I flew down the front steps to the waiting car.

My cousin had bed hair, a lit cigarette dangling from his lips, and the sort of squint people had walking out of a bar early in the morning. He looked like he hadn't showered in a couple of days. My eyes were swollen from crying. An hour before, my mom had finally called my aunt to wake him up. But none of that mattered now; he was here and he was mine for the day. After all my waiting and sacrifice, little could dampen the excitement. As soon as I slid into the car, I started complaining about all sorts of things that came to my lips easily. They were mostly grievances about my mother. How she wanted me to call my stepfather Dad but told me I had to behave myself because I wasn't his child. This dad would send me back to China if I didn't behave. I was looking for an ally, but when I paused to look over, my cousin just took another drag of his cigarette, his tired eyes on the road.

The lounge he owned was decorated in typical modern décor: leather booths along the back, padded steel stools, and blue fluorescent lights framing top-shelf liquor. He wiped the counter with a dark rag and lined up five shot glasses. I wondered what he remembered about me. I wanted to say something that would bring it all back, or at least break through the years. Anything. Before I could find the right words, Rose and Jess had arrived at my elbow. My cousin lit the shots on fire and we tossed them back, the hot liquid burning all the way down.

We didn't go fishing right away, and instead pulled up to a large rectangular warehouse. My cousin turned off the car and said he needed to pick something up from his mother. Trailing behind him down a long hall, I instantly recognized the buzzing from overheated sewing machines and the lint-filled air tickling my nostrils. It was a smaller factory than the one my parents owned, with only a handful of workers at their stations. No one seemed to care or notice my cousin and me approaching. We stopped in front of my aunt, bent over a mint-colored sewing machine. Her fingers continued to work while they talked, the needle head vibrating dangerously fast and millimeters from her index finger and thumb. Watching her hand made me queasy and I wanted to look away, but it seemed like something terrible would happen if I did. I stared until the needle blurred, my aunt's hands gently tugging at the fabric back and forth.

There was always talk of getting out of the business by my mother, my aunts, and our extended family. The Ace Lounge Bar was a step up from what his family was doing before, but my cousin, I found out, was still living at home. He'd stayed and I'd left. And while I convinced myself I had gotten away—from my desperate childhood, my constant inferiority, and the burden of immigration hardship—I could still see the needle vibrating over my aunt's coarse fingers and taste the impending dread, slick with alcohol in the back of my throat.

—

In college, I worked two, sometimes three part-time jobs. I never wanted to be in a position where I needed to ask my mother for help again. The job at the hibachi restaurant didn't last long. The restaurant business dried up during the off-season when students went home. I found another waitressing job, at a Vietnamese restaurant, close enough to walk from campus. When I moved off campus the second year, I applied to the department stores at the mall.

Only a few close friends knew the details of why I had no place to go during Thanksgiving, winter break, Easter break, summer break, and all the long weekends in between when school was closed. I was all too aware of all the ways I failed to fit in—the care packages my friends' parents sent during midterm week, visits over family weekend hosted by the college, vacations my classmates and friends took during the holidays and breaks. Unintentionally, my friends' close and picturesque families ostracized me further. The closer I lived with those whose lives I wished I had, the more I noticed the difference in how they had been raised. I was drawn to their large support systems, drawn to the confidence and security in their lives, drawn to their easy futures. Most of them did not work while in school, and even if they did, there was no pressure to make enough to support themselves. Soon my childhood and my relationship with my family felt like a secret.

While my classmates and roommates were on break, I started working in the kids' section at Sears. I worked my way up from the cash register to a sales role in the electronics section, where I earned commission. About a third of the employees at Sears were like me, students working through school, small-town kids going to the local community college and living at home. Another third were Sears veterans, some of whom had been there long enough to become managers and earn a salary with benefits. The rest, the last third, were just trying to make ends meet. They were permanent fixtures: moms, grandparents, retirees, and people who once thought they were only passing through. It was a miserable place, but more real than college in a way. The students at the university called the permanent residents in and around the Binghamton area "townies," but the townies were my coworkers and friends. When I was working at Sears, I could ignore everything, from the fact that my father died too young, to my mother excluding me from her family, and to my being orphaned during the holidays. The longer I stayed away, the more distant and irrelevant my childhood became. I was so sure I could forget it all. Before I knew it, I'd worked at Sears, selling sound systems, plasma TVs, and vacuum cleaners, for close to three years and graduation had arrived.

———

Five years after I left home and a year after I graduated college, my mother invited me back for dinner. It was a few days after Thanksgiving. She was a good cook now, she told me over the phone.

They had renovated the red-brick house like she said she would all those years ago. Even the entrance had been rebuilt—it now had two tacky Greek-style pillars. Inside there was a dramatic spiral staircase leading up to the second floor. The wall between the living and dining rooms had been knocked out and every piece of furniture was brand-new. I didn't recognize a single item.

They had redone the blue bathroom that I had watched Jill and Henry take baths in, where I washed my mother's bloodstained underwear, and where, when my mother was in a good mood, she allowed me to keep her company as she soaked in her nightly bath. Instead of powder blue, it was black and sleek with marble surfaces. The mirror reflected my stray hair and a startled expression.

As I walked around the house, the only thing I recognized was the shape of the kitchen. They had put in a sliding door between the kitchen and living room to keep the smell of food from traveling through the house. Now I smelled the warm fragrances of vinegar, dried mushrooms, and fried fish. My mouth watered with anticipation as I watched my mother at the stove. Hot-and-sour fish, Hong Kong–style lobster, marinated and cured meat, sautéed Chinese okra, minced pork with dried mushrooms, and a bone marrow soup with mustard greens.

I barely recognized Henry and Jill when they arrived at the dinner table. They had both shot up in height and developed their own styles. Puberty had changed their voices, given them adult bodies, but it was more than that, they had grown *into* themselves. They were like the house, a shadow, a reminder of what I once knew. I tried to catch glimpses of them, but they were attached to their phones. I didn't know how to speak to them. Was I their sister, a stranger, or something in between? I had not spoken to my stepfather since the night he sent me to the basement. He looked older, shrunken, and more weathered.

The savory dishes were difficult to enjoy with the awkward conversation. I searched for something to say.

"How's the factory?"

"Not great, it's hard. Gets harder to make the same kind of money every year," she responded.

I couldn't tell if there was any truth to what she said. It was the same answer I always got from her. I nodded and changed the subject.

After we ate, my mother invited me up to see the second floor. I had a flashback to the party she threw after I first got to New York. I was in a different role now—the guest. Instead of an office, my parents had turned my old room into a walk-in closet, which extended farther into their master bath. The loveliness of the heated floors and track lighting stunned me. There were dozens of Gucci and Louis Vuitton bags, multiple racks of color-coded suits, jackets, and miniskirts. A custom closet had been installed, with floor-to-ceiling drawers. It was meticulously organized and cared for, just the way she'd always looked after her possessions. It was all I needed to see to understand that it wasn't my stepfather's need or the world's need, but hers that left me without shelter, that left me feeling abandoned and alone.

"The floors are heated," she confided in me.

She seemed completely unaware of how the tour affected me. Maybe she had trouble figuring out who I was now, too, and how she should act toward me. Was I her guest who had never seen the renovations or the daughter she'd kicked out of her house? Next she showed me the bathroom, which had a porcelain bathtub and a standing shower. She proudly pointed to the his-and-hers sink. In the fancy new bathroom, all I could think about were the numerous breaks in school: Rosh Hashanah, Thanksgiving, spring break, winter break, and all the long three-day weekends in between. Rose or Jess would let me stay at their place for a week or two at a time, but it was not a permanent solution, and sometimes their families wanted to spend time alone with them. Holidays left me exposed in a way that I carefully avoided throughout the semester. I tried speaking with new friends, bringing it up casually, but they were all eighteen-year-olds, with no context for what I was asking. I could never stop feeling the shame of being a burden.

The solution came to me when I started dating a sophomore; I could stay with him in his apartment. I could hang out with him and his family to seem more normal and hide from the fraught imposter feeling that clung to me. I spent most of my college years with boys I tolerated so my mother could have a walk-in closet and a his-and-hers sink.

"What do you think?" she asked expectantly.

As a guest, I had missed my cue to say something nice.

I cleared my throat. "It looks great."

12

In 2012, my mother came to my first graduation ceremony. I was twenty-eight years old and getting my MFA. She came alone. My stepfather, having learned from Henry and Jill that I wrote nonfiction, was not coming, and neither were they. It made little to no difference in my life since we rarely spoke, I told myself, but I still cried after she told me. My mother showed up with an armful of red roses that were the largest I'd ever seen. She looked tiny and stricken in comparison.

She had taken a cab from Queens all the way to Westchester, a Jin Ma ride that cost well over a hundred dollars. I could see that she was shaking from nerves; she hated being in an unfamiliar situation. The day was a blur, and I placed her with my roommate's parents and joined in the row of smiling and overstimulated graduates as she told me the cost of her cab ride. I turned back to check on her just like my roommates with their families.

It was silly how deliriously happy I was. Maybe we had turned a new leaf, I thought. My mother—the only person I ever needed and wanted—was here at my graduation. It should have been too little, too late, but instead it felt like a dream I once had coming true. I felt like the rest of my classmates for once—with family in the crowd celebrating our achievements. I couldn't stop smiling as I looked around at the faces of writers that would go on to publish poems, chapbooks, essays, novels, and memoirs. Our futures felt equally bright for once.

After the ceremony, I took her to Underhill Crossing, a small restaurant in Bronxville where I was waiting tables when I wasn't writing or in class. She sat stiffly in her chair and left her menu untouched on the table.

"I'm not hungry," she said. "You order whatever you want."

I ordered a salad and fish tacos, not fully understanding her restraint until it hit me. She couldn't read anything on the menu. We hadn't gone out for a meal together in years, and never to a non-Chinese restaurant. I opened my menu again, rushing to explain each dish. How did you say *charred* in Chinese?

"This is for you," she said, abruptly, interrupting my description of the charred octopus appetizer I thought she'd like. She handed me a red box. It looked like all the Chinese jewelry boxes she kept in her ivory vanity table at home. Inside was an amber ring with a thick silver band. "It's the style you like, right? You are the first person in our family to graduate from college and now graduate school. I had to come today, even if no one else would come with me."

I knew education wasn't as important to our family as survival, as money, and in those ways, I had been rebellious, but I was surprised. How could I be the first one in our family to graduate from college? I wanted to ask about my extended family, all the cousins I was out of touch with. Their names were on the tip of my tongue, but I could only recall my cousin at the bar.

"Yes," I said, slipping on the ugly ring. "Thank you."

In my mother's eyes, I had beaten the odds. I was not like my cousins from China or my half siblings. I had charged ahead on my own and taken a path she could not have imagined for me. Maybe this was her way of telling me she was proud.

"*Cel-bry-tion*," she said in broken English.

Startup Life

13

In the summer of 2015, I start a new job. I am the office manager and the receptionist at a tech startup located in a new high-rise in Midtown Manhattan. My desk is situated near the office entrance, but if I squint I can make out New Jersey just past the sunny Hudson River. The skyline wraps around the open floor plan and the view reminds me of being on the City Wall in Xi'an, the way I was able to see miles of farming country extending to the airport, back in the direction of home. It's comforting.

The water glistens like shards of glass and my thoughts drift to my last conversation with my mother a month ago. We speak a few times a year over the phone. I asked about my grandparents. With me in America and them in China, the time we spent together became more irrelevant the older I grew. Over time, I moved on, accepting whatever morsels of information my mother offered.

"Your grandfather's gone," she told me over the phone. "You had work and I didn't want to trouble you. We went quickly. It was so hot, too hot and boring. You wouldn't have wanted to go all the way to China."

It took me a few seconds to parse through her meaning: my grandfather was dead; there had been a funeral in Wenzhou; and she had attended without me. She thought I wouldn't want to go because of the severity of the weather. I listened, stunned at the decision she had made for me. She must have received the news, purchased tickets, traveled seven thousand miles across the world, and spent a week or so in Wenzhou, before returning home to Queens. Was it two weeks, a month, or more since my grandfather's passing?

"We?" I asked after a stretch of silence. "*He* went too?"

"Well, yes, he's my *husband*. Of course, if I go, he will go."

My throat tightened. If I lost my anger, I would crumble, and I didn't want her to hear me cry. Anger was much more effective, much more acceptable with my mother. I'd forgotten she was like this—quick to pick my stepfather over me. The sharp edges of her words dug into a familiar scar, and an old, knowing feeling beckoned. *This was how it always was and how it will always be with her*, the feeling told me. It was an old childhood wound that had aired, healed, scabbed over, but here we were, picking at it again.

"I told you that if something happens, I wanted to . . ." I swallowed. "To say goodbye."

"Ai yo ah! Ni zao ke jou nio?" she asked. *Why would you go?*

When my father died and she left to begin a new life in America, Azi and Nie Nie took care of me. I slept between them. For those five years, I was more their child than hers, and she wanted to know why I would want to attend his funeral? Words failed me as the knot in my throat grew. As usual, her cutting tone made me feel small and worthless. I was submerged, drowned, and then put in my place. A hidden daughter with a dead father had no rights, not to say goodbye, not to attend a funeral.

I tried to recall Azi's face and bittersweet memories rose in its place. He didn't talk much and spent most of his day perched on a chair in front of the hardware store. Nie Nie cooked and cleaned in the kitchen at the back of the building, and Azi ran his business out front. He and I had chopstick fights over the last piece of pig's heart Nie Nie stewed in rock sugar. Playfully we vied for the final pieces of dried-mushroom meatballs and savory rice cakes. We were kids together, competing for Nie Nie's favor. He loved eating meat, smoking, and playing mahjong late into the night. I could still hear the click and rumble of plastic tiles mixing on an old mahjong table, noises that lulled me to sleep for years. I saw him under a cloud of cigarette smoke, the vice that would eventually kill him.

"The good news is Nie Nie will move here now that he's gone. You'll be able to see her," she added. "Think of how nice that will be when she's permanently living here."

I nodded, taking in her words. My grandparents represented a period of time before the red-brick house, before I understood what it meant to be lonely. In hindsight, there was a short window of my childhood that was happy and sheltered, and they had given me that. Everything after—living with my mother, being sent back to China, the four months at the sweatshop, and calling child services were years I wanted to forget. A secret we both harbored.

The conversation affects me for months. Guilt gnaws at me. I can't stop thinking about the time I'd missed with my grandparents, my aunts and uncles, and my cousins because it was easier that way. I relented when it meant less involvement with my mother. Now I look down at my laptop screen and search for and click on the New York Office of Child and Family Services website. The sidebar lists hotlines and toll-free numbers: Report Child Abuse & Neglect, Abandoned Infant, Domestic Violence, Justice Hotline, Foster Care and Adoption, and Child Care Complaint Line. Each iridescent button links to a subpage with a wealth of information, more leads, live links, a rabbit hole to explore. In an attempt to be comprehensive, they've overcomplicated the system. Still, it's more thoughtful than other government sites. After all, it's a place where most of the victims are children.

Victims. After fifteen years of being away from home and living on my own, the word still makes me uncomfortable, squeamish. The identity carries too much weight, too much shame. Not me! I wanted to shout. The amount of time I've spent in my mother's care is short compared to the years I've spent on my own, but they were crucial to who I am. After another few minutes of scrolling and clicking, I settle on: *If you were unable to find the answer to your question(s), send an email to OCFS.*

I compose a new email. My fingertips sweat over the keyboard. It's too quiet and I realize I'm holding my breath. I exhale, look out at the view, and let the air back into my lungs. The best part of this job is that on a clear day you can see past the Statue of

Liberty with her flame tirelessly held high, and even farther out, to a thin, translucent sliver of Staten Island. Underneath us, trees line up in a perfect rectangle around a crisp green lawn that looks pristine from the distance. Distance gives a different perspective, keeps us safe. Sometimes I press against the windows, ignoring my instinct to step back from the ledge, and stare straight down at the ant-size people. My fingers tingle and my breath fogs the glass as I imagine falling, the air pushing fast and hard against my face, my lungs ready to burst.

Being kept from my grandfather's funeral brings old feelings back, feelings of never being hidden enough, never being obedient enough, never being good enough. She didn't want me at a funeral where everyone could see the child she'd had from her first marriage. It's a fact I cannot change, but I am tired of keeping my distance. I want to unearth and understand what happened all those years ago. I'm ready to remember again. There is only one way to get a copy of my original record from OCFS and this is it—my way forward. I start typing, and without rereading the email, I send it.

—

Near where I sit, my coworker Cindy sits on a yoga ball that's supposed to work out abs and ass without going to the gym. She spends most of the day trying to stay balanced. Eli, our boss, is at a standing desk at the end of the row, wearing sneakers so worn the only white I see is his socks poking through holes in the top. There are only a few of us today, a ghost town of what was supposed to be an up-and-coming, successful startup.

Earlier this year *Fortune* featured our company on its unicorn list, a prestigious ranking of private startups with $1 billion valuations or higher. We ranked alongside companies like Uber, Snapchat, Airbnb, Pinterest, WeWork, and Dropbox. Yet up close, I already see the cracks in the infrastructure: the downsizing and attempts at subleasing the extra office space, the poor sales numbers, unpaid invoices, and company-wide freezes. Turnover and inconsistent cash flow are not rare in a startup, but I'm hearing forty people were laid off weeks before I joined. Only a dozen employees are left in New York, and no one has bothered to update our status with *Fortune*.

The phone rings and echoes through the deserted office. There are more than fifty vacant seats, and all my coworkers sit in two rows, across from and next to me. Instead of spreading out, we flock to the front of the office, toward the windows and one another. They can hear every call and conversation I have, and it makes me self-conscious and formal. I wait for the call to go to voice mail and then turn the volume down on the phone.

A few seconds later, the phone rings again. This time, a few heads turn my way. Reluctantly, I pick up. It's Fresh Direct calling to inquire when we will be paying our invoices. I suppress my annoyance and explain quietly into the mouthpiece how we're just waiting for investor funding. There's a pause on the other end as the guy works on his diplomatic reply. He asks me how long that might be.

"I've been told another week or so," I say. I leave out that I've been told that for over a month now and the answer was always the same. "I'm sure you know how it is with startups, our cash flow is always stop-and-go."

"I see . . ." the voice on the phone says, sympathetic and cordial. I'm beginning to resent the tone. "That's not a problem," he responds smoothly, "but since there are five invoices here, and it looks like we've been waiting for payment for four months, we will have to freeze the account in the meantime."

I sigh, think of what it will do to the already low morale in the office. I debate telling a lie and getting another week or two of credit. If our account is frozen, we will not have coffee, milk, sparkling water. Basic supplies for the office. Before I decide, he assures me that once payment is made, they'll be able to resume immediately with no delay. He hangs up and I'm left holding the phone. I don't like open floor plans, I decide.

The company is all smoke and mirrors. The sales guys are always closing deals, but the rumor is every contract is stuck at the same stage and the product isn't ready. They never move past the initial stage: launch. Bugs are still being worked out by our engineers and developers. And the technology is a bunch of ideas with mockups and fancy decks the sales team pitches.

The startup world is different from any other place I've worked. The industry pioneers new technologies and breakthroughs in science, and also lets go of traditional hierarchies. They are known for adopting flat organizational structures and open collaborative work spaces while cycling trendy perks. It's shiny and exciting, but faces problems that come from growing pains. They often lack process and follow-through. Their maturing, like an adolescent's development, often burns bright but uneven. For example, the allocations for many of the perks come from money that would have traditionally been put toward human resources, an employee handbook, 401(k)s, and better health-care plans.

This startup in particular allows for a type of illusion, a false sense of security that is unlike anything I've come across working in a sweatshop, a dentist's office, at restaurants, or in other office settings. We are in a stunning work space with the latest technology and electronics—I can see the stickers left on the fridge and the cabinets—and yet the reality is that the company can't pay the bills. Under the surface, it owes every vendor money. We have the appearance of a successful company, but instead of facing our problem, we're hiding it. It reminds me of my childhood; my mother's fear of losing her new family, and the pretense we went through to keep what we had. We were a middle-class family that dressed and looked the part, and yet she hid me. She sent me to work in a sweatshop.

I'm aware of the problem at the company only because money never lies. The lack of transparency from the headquarters in London makes me an unwilling accomplice. For more than a month now, I've been making the same empty promises to vendors that the company made to me, and when they broke their promises, I broke mine. They've compromised my credibility, made me into a liar. For now, it will all go: sparkling water, Terra and Kettle chips, Kind bars, fresh fruit, and milk. Unlike our Staples account for office supplies, frozen weeks ago, this cut will not go unnoticed.

—

One of the first surprises at the startup is seeing the complacency of my coworkers. I joined at the tail end of a massive layoff, and yet, when I talk to coworkers, we chitchat about their weekends and holiday plans. We talk about their kids, about sailing and the latest tech. No one broaches the instability or insecurity lurking under the surface, the invisible stress and pressure. Most of them probably thought we were getting in on the ground floor, the company was going to be the next Salesforce or Shopify. Some were even willing to ignore their intuition, overlooking flaws, the way the company threw money at problems.

Our weekly all-hands meetings are held in the conference room I now call Doom. My coworkers settle in and I stand. I don't want to be giving bad news, but if I have to, I might as well get it out of the way. Sweat collects on my upper lip as I wait for everyone to settle.

"We won't be ordering any office supplies or snacks until the company-wide freeze is over and the money comes in from investors. Cash flow, as you know, is a common startup issue and everything is fine, but there won't be any coffee, milk, sparkling waters, granola bars, or chips until ..." I lose my place when someone sighs and shuffles in their seat.

"It's going to be a lean budget for now. Let's not spend more than we need to," the COO chimes in. Eli is a company man, a born-and-bred New Yorker, who grew up with a strong, nononsense work ethic. He's a hard-ass when it comes to approving office needs and expenses, but a decent boss otherwise. Relieved to be out of the spotlight, I quickly take my seat.

"When are the expenses being reimbursed?" asks one of the

remaining sales guys. Most of the sales team has, on good faith, racked up thousands of dollars on their personal cards. There's a pause as we all sense the looming risk of putting work-related expenses on personal credit cards. We can feel interest accruing, doubt seeping in.

Eli turns out his hands in an open gesture before carefully collecting his words. It's the first time I've seen him hesitate in the months I've worked under him. It isn't his tech skills or leadership that make him invaluable to the company; it's his blind loyalty to the CEO. The noble quality seems like a handicap now, less admirable when the company repeatedly leaves us holding the bill. Good things do not always happen to those who work hard and follow orders.

"Look, it may be a while, but you'll be the first to be made whole," he says. "We don't know how long it will last. Everyone's gotta use their best judgment and do what's right for them."

And there it is, a brief wave of relief, as if we've all been waiting for this very conversation, and now that we've been told the truth, there's a reprieve. A break in the illusion. A cool mist on irritated wounds. The energy quickly shifts. We all feel it then—a single blow of regret. Months later, after the company files for bankruptcy, a few employees will gather and attempt to file a class action. Lawyers will tell them there is no merit to their case and no company to go after. Move on, they will say.

"Any other questions?" Eli asks, palms open again. There's a pained smile on his lips.

The narrative of success is a lie, and yet it's us, the workers, who are weighed down by the company's actions. We are the ones who define ourselves by where we work, our job title, how much we make, and what we do forty-plus hours a week. And now we are the ones that must pay the price for this attachment. One after another, we stand and trickle out of Doom in a single line, cattle to slaughter. We want to unknow Eli's doubt, to go back to his denial and the security of our ignorance. We want to go back to raging against the company's lack of transparency. We don't want transparency—some of us can't handle it. Now that we have this truth, what can we do with the information? What has it changed? It is as they say: there are no handrails in startups.

—

The report from the Office of Child and Family Services arrives via certified mail to my apartment in Brooklyn. I live with two roommates, so for privacy, I walk past the tiny kitchen to my bedroom. The room is so small my full-size bed touches three walls. I sit on it and run a finger along the ragged green-and-white edge of the torn stub and wonder how many hands it passed through. Who has seen it? Who received my request and approved it; who looked up and found the original report; who decided what sections to block out; and who finally made a copy and put it in the mail? I expected the process to be more rigorous, for there to be more bureaucratic hoops to jump through, but here it is, without much of a fuss or a fight, and now a pool of reserved energy stirs in anticipation. I marvel at the weight of what I'm about to learn.

The envelope tears just like every other piece of mail I've

opened. It's a minor miracle—that I should request information and have it arrive just like it was supposed to, right on time. The United States Postal Service at its best. My hands are sweaty and clumsy as I move to unfold the thick document. The pages are crisp and still stuck together, fresh from the printer. I take a breath that feels like an end and a beginning.

Half of all the writing is blocked out. I peel the pages apart. It's hard to piece together a narrative. I'm light-headed as I read between the blocked-out sections, looking for meaning in words, half sentences, trying to understand their assessment.

Then I am falling. Someone has tripped me and I am falling through the years of mistaken assumptions I've made since I was fifteen years old and Mrs. V. made the call. How many decisions were made based on the single premise that if you do the right thing, stand up for yourself, everything will turn out okay? That was the story the guidance counselor told me and the story I still tell myself. The papers I hold tell a different narrative. The Office of Child and Family Services, an institution shaped by federal laws and regulated by the state, ruled "No Abuse." My situation was not bad enough to intervene, pages and pages tell me. My childhood was as it should have been.

How could this be true? I want to hide, to unsee and unknow the letter. I lean back as waves of emotion trigger flashbacks.

At the age of nine, I loved drawing. My English was getting to a point where I generally understood what was happening, but I had difficulty communicating clearly. Drawing was an easier way of participating. I kept my colored pencils sharpened in a tin case my grandmother gave me, one of the few items I brought from China. When my mother came home one night, she had a question for me.

"Did you tell Jill she needs to ask to use your colored pencils?" she asked. My colored pencils rattled back and forth as I handed the tin over. I looked over at Jill, who had followed my mother into our room. "Answer me when I'm talking to you. Why are you looking at her?"

I turned from Jill to her, my chin tilted up. "It's mine. She needs to ask me to use it."

"Why would she need to ask you to use something that I bought?"

"You didn't buy it for me. Nie Nie did."

"Where do you think Nie Nie got the money from? You think she would have taken care of you for *free*?"

She handed back the small tin, the paint on the case peeled in speckles and slivers. I yanked it from her hands, and suddenly I was in the air. There was a rainbow of color: green, yellow, blue, red. My butt hit the carpet so hard I felt it in my tailbone.

From the floor, I watched her transform. She stormed to the open closet and grabbed a free metal hanger. The force of the wire told me I was no more than a piece of hide, cattle that needed to be broken. I raised my hands over my body, but it was useless. There was no choice but to crouch into a fetal position and let her have her way with the outside parts of my body. "You know . . . better than . . . to grab things . . . from my hand like . . . that!" She spat with each exhalation.

I thought of a myth then: a goddess on the moon. We prayed to her during the Mid-Autumn Moon Festival, and I thought if

I could escape, she might take pity on me. Take me in. Before I knew it, I was diving for the window—for the pale moon outside. My hands on the lip of the window, pulling, tugging, begging. It was simple: out the window was the only way to safety.

In my sureness, I forgot about the window screen. Just as I was about to pinch the corners of the childproof lock and lift, warm arms wrapped around my waist. My stepfather, appearing out of nowhere, yanked with all his strength. I flew for a second time that night, breathless until the floor knocked the air out of me. The only sound in the room was my mother's labored breathing. My rug-burned knees throbbed and my backside pulsed so hot I was afraid to move.

"Look at this. I can't be a part of this!" he shouted. I felt his arms move in the air again, in frustration this time, and then he stormed out.

When I tilted my head up to look at her, she was staring at me, her short bob disheveled, her nostrils flaring from exertion. There was a gleam of sweat on her brow.

"Look at what you did," she said just above a whisper, dropping the deformed hanger. The strength of her grip and the imprint of my body had changed the shape and the metal was crumpled into a grotesque piece of conceptual art at my knees.

The carpet swallowed her footsteps as she headed back to their bedroom after my stepfather. Everything burned then; my backside, my knees, my eyes, my face, my chest. I never touched those colored pencils again after that night.

—

I expected the truth to be in the paper I received, but all I feel is shame and disillusionment. This is not what I had been prepared to learn. I had wanted supporting information. She had been cruel and unfair to me, and therefore, I was right and she was wrong. I was looking for the lost childhood, the cheated years, but child services could not give me what I had lost. I shove the report into the darkest corner of my closet, hoping to deny the feelings that well up.

The system that is supposed to safeguard me did not believe me. I turned to it for help and it left me behind. In the next few days I think about justice and fairness. Who gets them from our system and why? I wonder if my family presented as middle class and the abuse was too well hidden. Was my case not "bad enough" for them to intervene? Was it because I was clean and fed? The OCFS left me behind like my father's death left me, like my mother's emigration to America left me. I am adrift, unmoored in a deep, sluggish despair.

I don't know to whom or where I can turn for answers. How do I reconcile what I read and what I felt to be true? I search online. From what I understand, reports of possible child abuse and neglect are received by child protective services and either "screened in" or "screened out." A report is considered screened in if there's enough information to suggest an investigation is warranted, and screened out if there's isn't. In the cases where they are screened out, the social worker may refer the person reporting the incident to other community services for additional help.

I find a report that says in 2006, an estimated total of 3.3

million referrals involving 6 million children were made by child protective service agencies, and approximately 62 percent were screened in and 38 percent were screened out. Was I part of the screened-out percentage? The more time passes, the angrier I get. The document doesn't change the fact that every day I lived in fear. It doesn't change the beatings, the neglect, the violence my mother enacted on my mind and body. It doesn't change the six months in China, the four months at the sweatshop, the ten years I lived with my family, but as another week passes, it makes me think differently of the world, of safety, and of what is tolerated.

What does the OCFS know about the truth? What do those people know about abuse? Fuck them. What did they know about my life? The system I turned to is ineffective, neglectful, and careless. I was wrong to call them, wrong to think they stood for justice and the safety of children, wrong to be naïve, wrong to be so idealistic. I was wrong.

—

I was only nine years old when I tried to jump out the window. The following day was a Sunday. My mother called me into her bedroom early in the morning. The room was immaculate as usual, and somehow seemed quieter than the rest of the house. My siblings hung out in their room every night, but I was rarely allowed in. Lancôme Tresor, my mother's perfume, hung in the air, a soft mist rising from the pink carpet. Any movement stirred the scent. Memories of my mother's rage, mingled with the scent, would ruin all perfume for me in the future. I hesitated at the door.

"Pull down your pants," she said. She stood in the middle of the freshly vacuumed room, a container of Vaseline in her hand, and nodded toward the bed.

I made no moves. It was hard to trust her kindness, especially with my eyes still swollen from crying the night before. "Quickly, come on." She tsked, her patience already gone.

I stepped in and her floral perfume escorted me to her bed, where I leaned over. The fabric rubbed painfully against my raw flesh as I pulled my tights down around my ankles. I couldn't see what she was doing as she lifted my shirt, but a second later, I felt the moist, cool touch of Vaseline, a calm reprieve for the angry cuts. We were silent as she gently dipped her finger into the jar and applied the jelly to my lower back, butt, and legs.

"You don't have the guts to kill yourself," she breathed, putting the cap back on and twisting it shut. She said it in a way that made me think she knew more about the subject than I did. It took guts I didn't have. I wondered how she knew. "All done. It's not bad at all," she said, tugging my pants up for me. Her tenderness was often short-lived and I didn't know how to respond quickly enough. I wanted to stay in the moment with her like this, calm, unthreatening, just the two of us.

"Do you want to paint your nails?" she asked, as if hearing my thoughts.

I averted my eyes and thought about her offer. She had never let me paint my nails before. Both my sister and I were not allowed to use makeup, wear heels, or paint our nails. On the left side of her white vanity bureau, she kept a dozen different shades of pink and red Essie nail polish. I touched them all carefully, turning the glossy bottles delicately in my hand. They rang like porcelain.

"Pick one," she said.

Overwhelmed, I let her pick a bubblegum-pink color.

She took the bottle from my hand and motioned for me to sit on the bed. Light poured through the shades and onto the duvet in angular streaks, like the keys of a piano. She held all my fingers in the cup of her hand and I watched the top of her head as she concentrated. I matched my breathing to hers, memorizing the moment, savoring and taking in each of her strokes.

When she was done, she let me jump around the room, flapping my arms like wings, a fledgling ready to leave the nest.

—

During stressful events, the stress response systems in the brain and body instinctually take over by overriding thinking and decision-making structures in the frontal lobes of the brain. The amygdala sends signals to the body as if it is in danger—even if there is no real threat. According to Pete Walker, a psychotherapist and writer, emotional flashbacks are a complex mixture of intense and confusing feelings, reliving of past childhood traumas. He calls these events "amygdala hijackings."

For me, an emotional flashback is like being dragged back to a traumatic moment and left with helpless feelings of sorrow, shame, and inadequacy. It strands me, leaves me crippled and submerged in a sea of numbness. Reading the document makes me feel like parts of me are being erased, silenced. As if what I went through could be denied, just like my mother had denied me as her child, denied my access to my family, denied closure after Azi's death. The fear and despair are illogical, but I can't make my way back. Sometimes having the language, and the education around it, is the only relief. I try to hold on to that knowledge.

14

I return after lunch in a park nearby to new rumors circulating. They don't have enough money to run payroll. An unsettled haze moves across the whole team, a brewing of foresight.

The next day a few people stop showing up to work. Some of us still want to believe the company will pull through, and it's hard to separate reality from our willful denial. Was there actually a chance or were we just irrationally hoping for the investors to save us? Were we gullible and naïve or calm and logical? In the coming weeks, sales, client success, marketing, and legal collapse to one single team. We all pretend to celebrate the departed and their good fortune, but there's a silent race to *not* be the last person left on the team. Our time will come, we assure one another, while widening our search and swallowing our own doubts. Maybe we're being too picky. We send one another job listings, apply to anything that sounds vaguely interesting or within our scope of skills. The camaraderie is strange, but sweet.

At the factory, if you knew the rules, you knew where you stood. You knew that if you punched in late, your rate for the day went down. The same was true if you punched in late from lunch. Generally speaking, if you kept up with everyone else, you'd get paid like everyone else. As poorly paid and painfully dull as it was at times, you had a job and the job was straightforward. It was exactly as advertised.

Here, in the startup world, rules are different. There is less clarity; you can work as much or as little as you want as long as you meet your bosses' expectations. Sometimes those expectations are sales- and analytics-related, and others, like in my job, are hard to pin down. My job is based on efficiency and budgeting, but also on the happiness of the employees. Sure, I can make sure the printer is working, the office phone is answered, snacks and beverages stocked, but can I keep people positive and engaged under the circumstances? Our company policy, typical of many startups, has a lax work-from-home policy, and unlimited sick and vacation days. Most of the employees never call out sick and work from home instead. Few people take more than a week or two of vacation. No one is really ever "off."

There are also expectations that you show excitement, passion, and commitment to your job. Call it an aspect of emotional labor: you are to market yourself, to be your own brand and present your best self. You are to love your job or at least like it enough to pretend to care. The pretense creates unrealistic expectations, isolation, anxiety, and stress.

Payday arrives and the rumors are true: no wages. No one knows what the right etiquette is in such a situation. We're angry, ready to fight for what is rightfully ours. We're up in arms, we complain, we talk shit, but deep down we feel abandoned and afraid. Two days pass and still we haven't been paid. We pull up our bank accounts on our browsers and keep them up, refreshing them every few hours. We don't care who sees.

The phone rings constantly. Contractors, vendors, and office suppliers call to yell, beg, or both. Usually after they are done, they threaten a lawsuit. I wonder why I am still putting up a brave front and answering the phone. Maybe I don't know any other way or maybe that's one commonality between sweatshop and startup labor—the loyal workers.

The loyalty expected at work is not so different from the blind loyalty of a child for their parents, at least not for me. Decisions are made for you, and if you misbehave, you get reprimanded. You are at the mercy of your employers, of your supervisors. They can control the information you have, use their position of power as leverage, manage you the way they please. To be a child is to be vulnerable, to be a worker is to be vulnerable. The uncertainty and the vulnerability in the office bring dread. Anger is not far behind, but what to do with the anger? The only person getting out of this unscathed is the CEO, who is merely taking advantage of the structures of capitalism. Those are not things I can change, but the blame comes back to me, to my inability to protect myself, to my inability to see through the illusions of the company earlier. A fire, an intense sense of unfairness and helplessness, reaching up from my belly.

I want this experience to change the way I work, to change the way I commit to an employer.

—

It is not my rage, but my mother's that hits me sometimes. An inheritance that the women in my family bear each day. We swallow parts of ourselves, instinctively neutralizing ourselves to fit the mold society has put us in. We are working women; women whose stories hold little value; women whose stories are not believed; women whose stories do not matter. All three generations of my family, starting with my grandmother (and probably going back further than that), were taught to be daughters, child bearers, caregivers, and laborers. Women born to carry more than their weight. Untethered anger stirs in all of us, and eventually becomes a tight ball of bitterness and resentment, handed down generation after generation. A rage that hides the fear of being forgotten, of being less than, of being obsolete. I can tell the weight isn't solely mine, the way I can tell when someone having a bad day suddenly snaps and transfers their mood to me. When it comes, it's a tidal wave, and the impact takes out everything in its path.

Perhaps the most infuriating and disappointing parts of the OCFS report are the inaccuracies: the careless misspelling of my name, the wrong number of hours I worked at the factory, the reason I spent six months in China, and finally, the sickening lie that my father was alive. From the redacted information, I can still make out that OCFS came by and interviewed someone at our house.

███████ parents are not mean to Ana. Parents treat all children the same. Ana biological father lives in China. Ana stayed in China during June, 1998-October. Ana returned to New York because she was involved with a male. ███████ parents buy food

Ana biological father lives in China. I can't tell if the interview was with Henry or my mother, the information is blocked out, but I do know that my father died on September 3, 1985, and I have the death certificate to prove it. To deny his death is to deny an essential part of who I am and the hardship I lived through. His death was the reason my mother left China alone, why I had been orphaned in China for five years, why I was inherently different from Henry or Jill. It's a type of silencing I have felt many times in my life, but for the first time, I see the injustice for what it is.

My mother showed me his death certificate years ago. She was cleaning out her closet, where she kept all her important documents, switching out her spring wardrobe, and I was helping fold clothes. I was barely a teen then, but I remember the cover of the multiple-page booklet was ivory and glossy, the surface silky against my palms. My fingers flipping through, combing the pages for a picture, something to hold on to besides the opaque and often shifting father figure I had in my head.

There was no photo, and the only splash of color was from the blood-red notary stamp. Two pages had writing on them; the first had a short paragraph in traditional Chinese, and the second page translated the first one into English. I stared at the words, line after line, willing them to tell me the story of who he was. It said he died in a traffic accident. I turned the page. There was no other information.

"I thought you said he died because of his head." I'd forgotten the word for cancer.

"He died of ———" She used a word for an illness I didn't know.

"But this says he died in a car accident."

My mother lashed out in anger whenever I brought him up, so I had never been able to fully understand how he died. For my entire childhood I'd thought he had brain cancer, and now I wasn't sure. She looked at me sharply, *tsssks* between her teeth. "Ah Na, they are all corrupt over there. You think he mattered? They write whatever they want in those things."

I bit my tongue, sat back on my heels, unsure who to believe: the government or my mother. Though no one in my family openly criticized the Communist country we came from, I knew we were here because of how things were there.

I wonder now if our two governments are more alike than I'd thought. One government had gotten the cause of death wrong, and the other one, the supposedly better government, thought he was alive. I can't believe the OCFS never verifies whether a parent is alive or dead. I wonder if Henry gave the interview while I was working at the factory. And if Henry *did* give the interview, he would have been no more than ten years old at the time. How could they have trusted a child?

The report does not have the answers I need. What I thought I knew at sixteen years old was a false sense of a perfect world, dreams Nie Nie weaved into my head that I kept for too long.

A better country, a better government. Now I see that the fundamental reasoning is flawed. Fairness doesn't apply to life. The expectation of justice is not a privilege with which I had been raised, and staring at the piece of paper, it occurs to me how black and white I have made my entire life out to be. I was going to get my justice; it was rightfully mine. How American of me.

—

An eviction notice arrives at the office in a plain manila envelope. The guy that hands it over says, "You've been served," just like they do on TV, before turning and walking out of the office without another word. The notice gives us twenty days to vacate the building before the doors are padlocked and our remaining assets confiscated.

The news sweeps across the office and takes up all the air. No one knew we had stopped paying rent. The wait and the ambiguity are finally over. Twenty days is aggressively short. A Band-Aid ripped clean off. The timing of our forced departure strikes me—a sinking startup, my grandfather's death, writing to child services, and now, an eviction. The seemingly coincidental combination is moving toward a single point, gathering meaning and significance just beyond my line of vision.

I was raised on the illusion of family, and that has led me astray—to cling to an illusion of success at work. I was an imposter in my home, and now I am working at a sham of a company. What does it say about me, my ability to recognize what's true and what's fake?

I can't help the mounting awareness that I am always situated on the edge of chaos. After we're handed the eviction notice, the day is a blur. We're all assessing our lives. Another thought comes to mind: What if I am putting myself in these situations just so I can survive them all over again? I'm good at coming out of difficult situations intact. Can I be partially responsible for landing in these situations, these cycles I can't seem to break? Abandoned by my parents, by the government, and now by this company, I can no longer ignore the connection. The chaos and distraction feel jarringly familiar. What if I am just a moth to flame? When I was working at the sweatshop, I thought I would be able to get away from my toxic home dynamic, from my abusive mother and the sweatshop work, but now I wonder if I carry that history with me wherever I go.

I'm on autopilot. I answer a few calls and they are all interchangeable in my mind.

"Yes, we're probably going under," I say to a vendor.

My coworkers' eyes remain on their screens and no one moves. Eavesdropping is for people who care, and we are no longer those people.

"You could and probably should sue us, but I'm not sure you'll get anything. Vendors rarely get money in the case of bankruptcy. Too low on the totem pole." I shrug as I speak into the phone. I wait a few seconds—let their shock register—and then hang up.

If I push past the feelings to what lies underneath, there's a cold, sobering voice. That voice whispers that I deserve to live in chaos, to be abandoned. I deserve only the life my mother forced me to live, and nothing more. I deserved the sweatshop, I deserved the shiny, hollow startup. If my own mother did not care about me, why would anyone else? If she didn't think I was worth anything, why would the world?

For as long as I can remember, my self-confidence was wrapped in what I could do for others. I worked at home, in a factory, at restaurants, at retail stores, at companies in various industries. That was who I was: a maid, a worker, a waitress, a cashier, an office manager. Who was I besides a useful worker?

My value in my family has always been as a worker. Family was business to my mother, and if I wasn't going to help her, then what use was I? What good was I to her if I didn't want to do chores, take care of my siblings, or work at the factory? Those were her lessons for ten years. It's the only validation I had growing up, and as I swallow the thought, I make the link to my value at work and my sense of value now. The old narrative is louder than any logic, sounder than any encouragement or denial. There is nowhere to run, no safety net, no family or work to shelter me.

—

In 2014, our startup self-proclaimed a valuation of roughly $3 billion. When investigated later, it was concluded that $100 million was a more accurate figure. The self-proclamation worked when it needed to, quickly drumming up media coverage, profile pieces. The media frenzy and inflated numbers also gave false leverage with investors.

The valuation of the company is part of the reason the owners are able to get away with what they do for as long as they do. The beauty of coming up with a product no one else has cracked yet is that no one challenges the company's financials or the promised product. It asks for more time to work out bugs and build functions, coming up with preloaded demos. It stalls, with confidence in its efforts to secure funding, find potential clients, and eventually sell the company.

Startups can and often do self-declare financial figures through arbitrary formulas, factoring in estimated future revenue, anticipated growth rates, and potential markets without any concrete facts or case studies. When I joined, the employees were still nostalgically talking about parties where supermodels dropped in on the arms of the CEO and the top executives. My coworkers told me stories of executives turning up with an assembly of good-looking sales guys ready to network and deliver pitches on a silver platter. I imagined that potential clients walked away feeling like they were in on a secret, and that was the best trick of all. Concrete business talks were a distraction, and real conversation was pushed off to a lunch meeting in the near future. The gatherings were extravagantly catered, and I heard stories of imported caviar, unlimited bottles of wine and champagne, revelry that lasted until the morning light stretched across the sky. By the time I joined, there were no wild parties, but the sixty-dollar bottles of champagne were still being served at events we never paid for.

Even with everything going on, the company tries to keep up appearances for as long as possible. First comes the downsizing, the frozen budgets, late payments, unanswered calls, and excuses. Then comes the slow internal communication; time difference is blamed, international legal difference is blamed, late investors are blamed. As long as appearances are kept up, there is still a chance to sell the company. But keeping up the illusion is out of their control now. Someone discovers that this isn't the first company led by our CEO to go bankrupt, and rumors circulate that he is keeping any technology and innovation we've developed and selling it to himself. We feel that he's getting away scot-free, while the rest of us find ourselves without jobs, without pay.

A few days later, we're called into the Doom room for one of our last meetings. We're all on edge. *What if the paycheck never comes this time?* No one speaks as we file in, mentally preparing for what will come. If the rumors are true, then this will be the second late paycheck in two months. The video plays on the still-new sixty-inch TV; we scoff at the irony.

Our CEO looks exactly like every other time I've seen him. He wears a dark pin-striped suit, and his hair is slicked back with too much gel. The one and only time we met, his eyes lingered on my legs during our introduction. He starts by thanking us for our dedication and faith in the company. I look over just in time to see my coworker Gina rolling her eyes.

"It has been a tough few months, but good news is coming," he begins. To show his appreciation, he's giving us all a bump in the next paycheck. He's also working on the investors to get payroll on time, but it may be a couple of days late. The video is short, barely seven minutes long.

"He didn't even have the guts to tell us on a call. It had to be a video! Coward," Gina mumbles, before switching to an insult in Italian. I realize she's right; a video seems more official, and less open to discussion. No one can ask questions or make comments. And worse yet, it forces us to face our helplessness, our lack of choice. There is only silence as we walk back to our desks.

In 2015, about 90 percent of startups fail. Employees, contractors, vendors, and small businesses pay the price. Once a company files for bankruptcy, it is let off the hook. Everyone else eats their losses.

Right after the startup filed for bankruptcy, a trade magazine revealed that most of our "contracts" had, in fact, been nonbinding letters of intent. Without a finished product, they meant nothing.

—

With the company's lies exposed finally, the office walls are bare within a week. Within days of the eviction notice, my coworkers start claiming items—the big-screen TVs in the conference rooms, the extra laptops, monitors, tablets, and smartphones. Every day something else is lifted, looted. The reception chair, the rug, a fake plant we purchased when we could no longer afford fresh flowers. The only things no one touches are the office supplies: notebooks, Post-its, dry erasers, Sharpies, pens, paper clips, and reams of paper. Those items remain until the end.

A month has passed since we were paid, and we're feeling emboldened. What is left in the office is ours and no one can tell us otherwise. Screw the CEO, screw the company. The only sales guy left takes one of the two egg chairs by the waiting area and I quickly tack a Post-it with my name on the other. When in Rome and all. We're abandoning ship, salvaging what we can before the building bars the doors and confiscates it all.

—

My grandmother lies, my mother lies, I lie. Lies were necessary in our family. It was survival, or at least that was the excuse. Throughout my childhood, my mother rarely invited guests over, and when an unexpected visitor stopped by the house, she hid me in the basement. I would leave my food half-eaten, still warm, and run to the washer-and-dryer room. It told me that whoever was visiting had no idea of my existence. I sat on top of the hot dryer, waiting for the end of the cycle, waiting for my mother to send Jill to tell me I could come back. My mother had the power to erase my existence with her lies.

I wanted to see the truth. I wanted out of the shadows, and true to my upbringing, I thought force was the way. I thought I could force her to change, make her see that I was as valuable as my half siblings. Calling child services was about standing up for myself and how I wanted to be treated. It was about a higher authority coming to tell her to treat me with love.

One of my first memories is my grandmother telling me about the life waiting for me in America. Nie Nie told it like a fairy tale; full of playtime, visiting parks and toy stores, bicycles and sweets. I wanted to go back to that place, a place with a distant mountain full of longans and peach trees nodding in the wind, my grandmother whispering hope in my ear. It was easier to live there, in a land of magical thinking, dreaming of a kinder destination. I missed her.

Instead this is my reality. They did the right thing to leave me with my mother. The OCFS could have taken me and put me in the foster system for two years before I turned eighteen, but that would have been the riskier choice. I could only imagine the untold horrors I might have experienced in such a place. My home was not ideal and I was unhappy, but most of the damage had been done, and to transition to a third situation at sixteen years old would have been a worse fate. The truth is, living in an uncomfortable house where I was not wanted trumped any foster home or youth housing program. There was food, clean clothes, and no clear evidence of violence or abuse, and that was good enough. But when all is quiet, I am left facing painful questions. Was I abused at all? By whose definition and what authority do we define abuse? Does it matter? I don't know if I'll ever find the answers to these questions.

—

On my last day, I carry the egg chair from the reception area to the freight elevator with the help of a coworker. I've never allowed myself to grieve for my grandfather's death and my mother's rejection—now seems as good a time as any. As my coworker and I drag the gray egg chair into the freight elevator, I find myself wiping tears from my face. It's as if I can't get away from where I've always been; my father's tragic death; my mother's shame and duty; my unhappy years in the red-brick house. I have no father, no mother, no family, no safety net, and now, no job. Soon I will file for unemployment for the first time in my life. Shame washes over me at the thought, like when my mother talked about the money she'd spent on me, wasted money, money she'd never get back.

On the street, we shudder against the breezy evening. The Midtown skyline grows brighter as we wait, our arms wrapped around our shoulders for warmth. We're in among a number of skyscrapers and there's no cover from the wind. We all feel, to an extent, an exaggeration of our own struggles. Our story feels like *the* story, and even when we know that we experience it as hyperbole, we cannot save ourselves from the feeling that everything will collapse under its weight. The pressure is infinite and the anguish unrelenting, and all we can do is push through and keep going. Getting from point A, where we see only ourselves, to point B, where experiences are profound and still ordinary, is a leap, not a continuum. Our existence, the current and impending dilemma, contains us and it is only in slivers of awareness that we are able to see things as they truly are. On such a night, it is easier to see how temporary work is, whether working at below minimum wage in a factory or being paid a salary at a startup. I look up at the almost dark sky, for stars hidden from view. I think about the factory work, the startup, all the jobs that came in between, and wish I could separate myself from them. I want to be me instead of the work I do.

By the time a black SUV pulls up, I have decided I am over startups. I need more stability and transparency. I want a permanent job where the company puts policies and regulations first, one that respects laws meant to protect and serve employees. The market is saturated with jobs at startups, but I'll navigate around them. I'll keep searching for a better way to work.

The driver gets out to help us load the chair despite the disgruntled cars that honk at us. We're in a no-loading zone and causing congestion. The three of us focus on the task at hand, ignoring all our other senses, shifting the armchair around and around and around until it sits just right. Only then is it done. Only then does the trunk door shut, and we climb in.

Burning Paper Money

15

In May, a full month into unemployment, I go with my friend Amanda to see a play in the East Village, called *Midnight Kill*. Theater for the New City is old, and each auditorium seats more people than feels comfortable. The play opens with the murder of a woman by her lover in bed, and then his confession. Set in 1970s China, it follows the lives of a handful of teachers in a mountain village—Li and Mei, the protagonists, among them—and the challenges they face in the harsh, ascetic climate of the Cultural Revolution. We find out universities have stopped enrollment, students of primary and secondary schools are forced to study Mao Zedong Thought as a majority of their curriculum, and the invisible "Big Brother" covers the entire country, brainwashing one half and silencing the other through fear and paranoia, creating a split reality.

Mei's husband is impotent, yet his family expects an heir. She solicits an affair with another teacher, Li. For each child she has, she will get a monthly allowance that is double what a teacher makes. When Li discovers the depth of Mei's calculated manipulation and her unconscionable use of childbearing, he kills her in a fit of rage.

At intermission, Amanda and I purchase tea in flimsy foam cups and huddle over the steam, silently soaking in the desperate and stark plot of the play. I am in a daze. I can't retain anything Amanda is saying to me, and she stops talking after a while.

Oppression and survival drive the characters to want for basic human needs. As the story unfolds and becomes more complicated, I begin sweating. I can't understand how I stumbled across something so personal without looking for it. My mother rarely spoke about her childhood directly, but I know all her actions are motivated by her experiences during her childhood. The story and timeline are eerily similar. Mei's language, idioms, sense of humor, justification, and reasoning bring me back to my mother and her sacrifices for survival and class mobility. The unceasing hunger and desperation are familiar to me. Loved ones pay the biggest price. The room is as silent at the end of the play as it was at the opening murder scene. No one dares to take their eyes off the stage. We're watching ghosts we recognize.

I stay and listen to KK Wong, the writer and director, take questions. He tells us the play is based on a real story. It is set in a town only a couple of hundred miles from where my mother and I were born. I want to cry for the characters, for my mother, for all of us in the audience that bear witness and mourn the generations of trauma handed down. I am beginning to realize that we are all raised by children. Children that are shaped by their own traumas, some of them unable to forget or overcome what happened to them before they passed it along.

As we bundle back up to leave the theater, I think back to Mary. It's been years since I've thought about her, but one of my sessions comes back to me now. We were sitting in the living room. Prefaced with a tired sigh, she said it wasn't just hard for me, it was difficult for my mother, too. *She has her reasons*, she said. I didn't know what she meant. I was fifteen, in tears, and everything that seemed wrong with the world began and ended with my mother. She was the mean parent, the one who made all the rules, the one that separated me from the family, so how could it be hard for her? She was the supreme authority. I was so sure she was creating all my problems and refusing to be a better mother to me. It did not benefit her to treat me with compassion and decency, so she didn't. That's all I needed to understand of her reasoning.

I was on the edge of what I didn't want to know. I was afraid of Mary's response, of what she would tell me that might ruin my perspective and take my rage. I needed a villain, and there was no better villain than the person that abandoned me over and over again, a person that was supposed to protect and care for me. Instead of understanding this, I chose to take it as a betrayal on Mary's part—she didn't understand me, or what I was going through. There was Mary, inserted into the middle of a torrent, holding on to both of us, one on each arm.

I didn't want to know what she meant, and she didn't push the conversation.

My mother's goal in life was like that of many immigrants. She wanted an easier life with more opportunity for herself and her family. A life filled with enough food, a comfortable home, and children that behave. Beyond that, she hoped her children would have the opportunity to pursue careers they wanted, a chance at a fuller, happier life. She wanted them to simultaneously appreciate the hardships she faced, to never have to fully know those cruelties, and to be grateful for the opportunities they'd had. An impossible number of contradictions, but a common one among immigrants.

In her daring ascent to the upper middle class, there was a residual, telling effect of poverty in the way she kept the fridge and cupboards overstocked, in the way she relished and lauded simple foods and showy gifts. There was almost a reverence for jewelry, clothing, and high heels that revealed deeper meaning than the objects alone. They were symbols of her achievement. She could not leave the house without her hair blown out, her face made up, diamonds guarding her collar, and a Louis Vuitton bag in the crook of her arm. They were her protective armor as well as the fruits of her labor.

There was nothing she'd kept from her old life in China, no single article of clothing, no piece of artwork or memorabilia, no sentimentality. She eradicated it the same way I learned decades later to eradicate my Chineseness. Her marriage with my stepfather is ever important—the distance she traveled reinforced by the choices she's made. Keeping anything from a time before him was betrayal, she once told me. I thought of the past that must haunt her and her conviction to move forward.

—

After missing my grandfather's funeral, it takes me over two years to return my mother's calls. The time passes quickly. Where most people think of family on Thanksgiving and Christmas, most of my guilt peaks around Mother's Day and her birthday in November. "Wei? Happy Mother's Day," I mumble obligatorily when she picks up. I take short, cautious breaths, knowing she's pissed off. "How are you?"

"I'm always the same," she says, her voice strained. "I'm fine."

I do what I always do, and explain myself in broken Wenzhounese. "I was really ... upset you didn't tell me when Azi died. I really wanted to go to his funeral."

I search for the word for closure, to explain what it meant to me, but I can't even remember the word for goodbye. "Zeibei ni," she bites back. Her voice, uneven and thin, painful to listen to. *Whatever you want.* "You're an adult, right?" she says, her anger barely contained. "You can call me when you feel like it. But you know what, I'm not going to worry about you. You do what you want, call when you want."

My impulse is to apologize, but I can see down that path and I know where it leads. I close my lips and resist the urge, tuck the apology under my tongue. It's better to live in discomfort than to go back. I still don't know why she went to my grandfather's funeral without me when I'd explicitly expressed my desire to go. Maybe it would have meant traveling to China together and bringing me back to the place we were both born. She couldn't handle that. So instead of dealing with the truth, she did what she always did. She buried her head in the sand and did what was best for her. Considering our strained relationship, maybe it was an impossible ask from the beginning.

How does one change their relationship with their mother? How does the child guide the relationship away from how it had always been? I want a better dynamic, but I'm at a loss. All I have is the idea of the mother I wanted her to be. There were the expectations that I always imposed on her and the expectations she had for me, and I didn't know how to break through that barrier.

My mother, the youngest of five siblings and malnourished since the womb, can't let go of the desperation of her youth. Often little more than watery rice porridge with a fermented turnip or broccoli root fed her for days. Meat and eggs were a rarity, and with four siblings under Mao's reign, it was uncommon to finish a meal and feel full. But everyone suffered, and to complain was to acknowledge she had it worse than others, which she could not do. Everyone had their difficulties. It would be a selfish, undignified act to argue her singular struggle. But at what point are we responsible for our actions? At what point are we no longer children?

"Is that all?" she asks, showing an unfamiliar restraint. "Is there anything else? Anything wrong?"

"No, nothing is wrong." I haven't seen her for years, but I try to picture her now. She didn't eat much, but it gave her peace of mind to be surrounded by snacks in the pantry, meat in the freezer, and leftovers in the fridge. If you asked her, she could quote how much she paid per pound of pork, dried shrimp, Chinese vegetables, or fruit. Her bones were steeped in hunger, and no matter how much food she bought or how much she put into her body, an empty space remained. It made her hard and sharp, like the tip of a butcher knife, waiting for a bled-out animal to arrive on the cutting board.

I can't see all the ways it has shaped and conditioned me, but her hunger and anger are in me. We are the same, and that is why neither of us can give way to the other.

"Okay, you don't have to call if nothing is wrong."

"Wuo ja," I say, suddenly drained. I want to fix us, but I don't know the way. "Happy Mother's Day."

I hang up only to realize I had forgotten the goal of the call.

—

One night while I was a teenager, my mother approached me with some news. I was recycling my stepfather's empty beer bottles in the garage. Her shadow came up behind me first. Light filtered in from the kitchen and her shadow joined mine. We were two heads sharing a monster-size body.

"Nie Nie went up the mountain to get your fortune read."

"Why?" I asked, turning around to face her.

She sucked in a breath between her teeth. *Tsssk.*

"Because that's where the best ones are," she said impatiently. "She said you were a bad man in your last life."

"I was a man?" The news made me want to giggle. I couldn't imagine myself a man, never mind a bad one.

"Now you have to pay for it in this lifetime."

"What did I do?" I imagined myself a man pillaging and raping villages on a horse. Maybe I burned down towns, maybe I was a samurai roaming from village to village for assassination jobs. Did China have samurais or was that Japan? Was I Chinese in my past lives?

"You were a thief and a gambler, and a drunk," she said flatly. "The fortune-teller said the first eighteen years of your life will be difficult and then it will get better. Your grandmother paid your debt off."

I stared at our feet and followed the shadow that linked us together. I was sixteen years old, so I had two more years. What did it mean that she was telling me my life would be most difficult while living with her? I wondered if she was the messenger or the gatekeeper.

"How did she know how much money I owe? How did she pay it?"

"By burning paper money."

Even in death, money was necessary. I'd seen money burning only at Buddhist funerals or grave sites. Fake money, thin red and yellow tissue paper with gold writing, was sold in giant stacks and burned in buckets. Ceremonies were accompanied by monks chanting, mourners crying, food placed at altars for the gods, and plenty of incense to carry prayers. I didn't realize you could burn money to pay off a debt from a previous life, but that made about as much sense as other traditions.

Only when she was gone did I gather that it wasn't just my fortune, but hers as well. We were both counting down the years.

—

With Azi gone, the urgency to connect with Nie Nie is a constant worry. I call my mother again a few weeks later, determined not to hang up without a clear answer about my grandmother's whereabouts.

"Why are you calling me?" she asks when she answers.

I clear my voice, and get to the point.

"Is Nie Nie here? In America?"

"Hmm, with your aunt."

"I want to see her."

"I'll tell her the next time I see her."

I want the conversation to last longer, but I have nothing to offer. I'm aware she may not do what she's promised and I have no way of appealing to her.

"Is that all?"

A month passes.

—

Bonnie, my therapist, once told me that intention counts only in action. I'd been seeing her for years by then, but I still didn't want to believe her. I started thinking about intentions when I was eighteen, the age my mother had me. Every year I put myself in her shoes and thought about how difficult it would be to raise a child. My child would be two, five, eight, fourteen years old now. A teenager with needs and wants of her or his own. Would I have been a better mom? Was it even a fair comparison considering the opportunities I had grown up with, the world I lived in? I thought about the good intentions she must have had when she was pregnant, how quickly it soured with my father's illness, like quicksand threatening to drag her down with him. It was two decades after the Great Famine, but food was scarce and surviving was still a fear in people's minds. Unlike now, the middle class was small, practically nonexistent in Communist China, and our family was as poor and uneducated as they came. After his death, my mother and I quickly began to go hungry without support.

The only story my mother liked to tell was about a time she asked for help after my father's death. She cleaned and dressed us in our best clothes, and carried me in her arms to my father's brother's house. She wanted to put me in front of them—a still-bald fifteen-month toddler—so that they could see we were both going hungry. She hated asking, but if she was going to ask, she wanted to make it difficult for them to say no. At their house, they wouldn't see us right away, and we waited at the entrance in the hot sun. When they finally greeted us, they said they were struggling, too, and didn't have much. There was a bowl of bananas on their table and I reached for one. They pulled it from my hands. We left with me crying and without being offered a glass of water, she always noted.

My father's death branded her a bad omen. Who would want to marry someone whose husband died within the first two years of their marriage? And even more to the point, no one would want to take on another man's responsibility. Under China's one-child policy, my mother had already had her child. Gathering all of her resources from my father's older sister, the only relative with any sympathy for us, she got her papers. It was her chance to leave behind the brutal hunger and judgment. All she had to do was leave everything she knew.

Eventually, my mother came to work at my stepfather's factory in Long Island City. She was one of the women on the sewing machines. She boasts she had the quickest hands that my stepfather had ever seen, and it was her work ethic that caught his attention. Even then, she was who she is now: a planner. Her intentions were an arrowhead she sharpened day in and day out, aligning reality to her will until I was in front of her again. Work hard, make money, get married, have two children (at least one boy), buy a house, and go back for your daughter. It was only after the arrow hit its mark, and I arrived at the steps of my new home, that the situation grew more complicated. Perhaps she hadn't thought further than that.

After years of Nie Nie whispering how grand America was going to be, I arrived with a list of expectations. I had high hopes of spending quality time with my mother, making meals, staying home, shopping, and learning English. I made a list of things we'd do together, things kids in the neighborhood back in Wenzhou did with their mothers. I must have sensed I was losing somehow. Where was the mother I was promised?

Intention is a lodestar, a guiding light toward an illusion. It doesn't matter if intentions are measurable, I still wanted to believe they color everything they touch. Follow them like a stream of water, back to its source and its once intended path. I wanted what was owed to me, and in order for that to exist, I needed to believe in her intentions even if no one else did. It was my job to keep them alive now that Nie Nie could not whisper dreams of a better life in my ear. If I didn't, then I would truly be the orphan all the kids called me.

—

The next time I call my mother, she lets the phone ring, and then calls me back twenty minutes later. She has one tone with me.

"Nie Nie is old now and doesn't think much of the past. Don't bother her with this stuff."

I ignore the heat rising to my cheeks and swallow the humiliation of being "this stuff." I grit my teeth and press on. "Can I have her number? I can call and ask myself. If she doesn't want to see me, I won't bother her again."

She *tssks* between her teeth.

She pauses, weighing her words. "I can't just give you her number like that. I have to ask if it's okay first."

It takes me a moment to soak in that she is angrier than she's ever been with me and is choosing to make this difficult. I wonder if she's mentioned me to my grandmother at all. Or if this is another punishment I must endure. I'd dodged her calls for two years now and just because I am ready to talk again, she may not be. She has not agreed to mend our relationship, and with each passing conversation, I am becoming more aware of what remained unsaid. It doesn't make sense that my grandmother wouldn't want to hear from me.

"Wuo ja, will you call me back after you ask her?"

"I'm busy right now," she says evasively. "Maybe I'll call her in the next few days."

We are not a forgiving breed of women.

—

Another couple of days pass, a week, and I feel frenzied. I call her again. She yells and says she hasn't had the time. I'm relentless, she tells me. She can't believe I'm like this.

A few days later, I get a text. There's a phone number. I text back, *Thank you!!*

I jump up and down until my head is spinning. I call two of my closest friends and scream into the phone. They can barely understand me. None of that matters because I finally have a way to reach Nie Nie.

It takes an hour to collect myself before making the call. There is no answer, it goes straight to voice mail. I try two more times and get a Chinese operator telling me no one is available to receive my call. I leave an awkward voice message. With the help of Google Translate, I put the last twenty years into two simplified Chinese sentences. There's no response.

I wait. I can't remember if my grandmother can read. Does she know how to access her voice mail? I shower and sleep with my phone close by.

I think about my promise to my mother. If my grandmother

doesn't want to see me, I will stop bothering her. Was this that? The seed of doubt my mother left makes me hesitate, keeps me calling in moderation. Had my mother told my grandmother not to answer my calls? Did she not want to speak to me? The shame is too much to bear, and I lose the confidence to call.

—

Over a weekend, between calls to my grandmother, I visit Flushing. The trip from Brooklyn is only about four miles, but it takes well over an hour. The 7 line has newer rail cars than when I was fifteen years old, but it's just as packed as when I commuted to the sweatshop. I avoided this train for a long time and rarely go to Flushing. I felt watched, afraid someone might recognize me and report back to my mother. Shaking off the feeling took too long, and usually, it wasn't worth the journey. This visit was different. I had made the choice to take the trip, and having a choice changed things.

I want to bring home the flavors of my childhood: the familiar tartness of pickled daikon, the saltiness of dried croaker, and the particular stink of fermented tofu. When I visit Chinese grocery stores, I naturally think of my mother. It's one of the few places of which I have good memories. A few blocks from the train station, I roam the aisles at Hong Kong Supermarket. I pass the fresh tanks filled with fat tilapia, lazy lobsters, and other water creatures. A butcher shouts out a number and I pass into an aisle of dried seafood. The rows are lined with familiar packaging and products. Stuff my mother and I love. Large dried shrimp, octopus, stingray, sea cucumber, and scallops that, once rehydrated and added to stir-fry, make the best comfort food.

I pick up a packet of small dried shrimp and bring it up to my nose. I close my eyes and inhale deeply. I look at the price, $7.99 for 3 oz. As an adult, I'm cognizant of how expensive it is to provide for a child and how much work it is just to support myself. Even with a full-time job, I can barely pay rent and all my bills. There's always something else I need to pay for, another cost that needs covering. *Prices are going up*, my mother always lamented. She was right about a lot of things. I add the package to my cart.

I call Nie Nie's number again and, as usual, it goes straight to voice mail. I chew on the inside of my lip and dial my mother.

"Is there another number for her?"

"No, that's the number. I don't have anything else for you," she says defensively, before adding, "Keep trying."

She hangs up.

I try calling the number early in the morning, and then late at night. Sometimes it rings once and then dies, other times it keeps ringing and goes to an automated Mandarin recording.

After therapy one day, I try calling in the middle of the day, and out of the blue, like a hand reaching through the dark abyss, she answers.

"Wai?" Nie Nie says.

16

We weep when we see each other. Nie Nie pulls me into her bedroom as soon as I take off my shoes. She lives on the first floor of a three-story apartment building my aunt owns in Jackson Heights. The furniture is sparse: a black leather couch, a mahjong table, a piano, and a TV. There are no personal items, no splashes of color, and no art on the walls. It's a place of necessity. There's only one chair in her room and I have her sit. I take the floor. She reaches for me over and over, tears streaming silently down the valleys of her worn face. I give her both my arms. I get my need for physical affection from her, I realize as I pat her arm. Joy makes our faces sore and tight, bursting with bright tears. Joy is harder to hold back than pain.

At eighty-three, Nie Nie is in good health, but has trouble getting around on her own. Her frame is small, her body round and soft. Her face is the same, just under a few more folds of wrinkles. She has become pale in sedentary life. I remember her bronze skin—hands that were always cleaning, fussing, nudging, yanking, hauling, tugging, and slapping. Active hands that kept us clean and fed, and taught us manners. I remember her chasing me, her legs faster and sturdier than mine. She can't run any longer, she tells me. I'm grateful for the years I spent with her and for how much they shaped me. I was fortunate to have known her love before I lived with my mother, before entering my complicated family dynamic, before understanding what that would mean for me. For the first time, I wonder if it was a blessing to have arrived ignorant of what my life would hold for the next decade. I can see that the way my grandmother taught me to dream saved me.

"I've been so worried. Every day I think about you. Have you eaten? Were you warm? Every day I worried about you. I never knew these things," she sobs.

"You don't have to worry about me, Nie Nie, I'm fine. I'm an adult." I smile and then add, "It's been a long time since I worried about those things."

I'm surprised at how true those words are.

"Look at these photos. I always kept them by my bedside."

She hands me a faded envelope with three photos inside. They are all of me, at two, four, and six. There's a familiar Polaroid of the three of us, Azi, Nie Nie, and me. We're standing in front of the Forbidden City in Beijing. I am on my grandmother's hip. I know the picture: it was when my mother left us for America.

"Every day I looked at them. Look at how torn the corners are."

"Azi was so handsome," I say, turning the photo over to see if there is anything written on it.

She chuckles and rubs her right knee, the one that's been giving her trouble lately. "I never thought I'd see the day. Buddha has eyes." She raises both her hands toward the sky in a prayer for the second time. Her voice cracks as she thanks Buddha. "He has given you back to me before it was too late."

I've forgotten how religious she is. Certain things are coming back, but not in the way or order I expected them. I can feel her affection for me even though she has no idea who I am or who I've been for so long. It simultaneously feels like I've been the same person since I was seven years old, and like none of what came after mattered. Whoever I choose to be, she would love me. I am struck by the enormity of it. It's the feeling I've been searching for, the unconditional love I've been trying to pull out of my mother for close to twenty-five years. The moment of clarity is an everything kind of feeling; a quiet, peaceful lifting, like having the space in the room to breathe, to be myself, to be loved.

I'm struck by the immediate intimacy between us. After twenty-five years, there's still a natural closeness with my grandmother that makes certain things stark about my relationship with my mother. We never had this easy attachment, this kind of open conversation, the warmth. It is clear that the role I expected her to play was not one she wanted to fulfill. For the first time, I am ready to see that perhaps my mother is not capable of loving me the way I needed. I had wanted her to replace my grandmother. She was to live up to a love that was fierce, generous, and unconditional. Holding Nie Nie's hands, I see what I've truly been fighting for all these years.

Time has returned to us in an unexpected way. Her sharp, fluid memory pulls one story after another, so much so that the years begin slipping away as I listen to her. Her neck lengthens, her wrinkles disappear, and the color returns to her tearstained cheeks. I lay my head on her lap and glimpse another uncomfortable wisdom. I see her austere, difficult life, the sturdy patience and familiar endurance. Sacrifice is in every generation of our family. I am no exception from the hardship, and we are all her children.

—

"Why didn't you ask my mother for my phone number?" I ask finally.

She gives me a sideways look, a shake of her head. Her expression tells me there is a lot that cannot be said. "She didn't offer and I didn't ask."

I open my mouth to reply. I wanted to ask how that could be. My mother is her daughter. What could not be offered or asked? But I remember something else: mother-daughter conflict is not new in my family; and in just a few words, I have more insight into their relationship than I was prepared for. What happened between them? I feel powerless on her behalf: the powerlessness of old age and the powerlessness of being a child are similar. I nod instead, accepting her version of the truth and allowing her answer to be enough for the time being.

"I've been trying to find you for years. She told me you didn't want to see—" My voice breaks before I can finish. She pats me again and nods.

She points out the neatly made bed, the walnut wood dressers and cheap plastic curtains. "Your mother bought them. To me, she's generous."

She's proud of how far my mother has climbed, for how much she's helped her family, and her filial piety. My mother has supported her the most among her children, she tells me. My mother's success is her success. And at the same time, she is not surprised by the way my mother treated me. She pats my hand and shrugs. "I was ruthless, too. I used to beat my kids senseless. That's how it was then, mai."

For a moment, I want her to say something about my mother's actions, about her selfishness, about my childhood, but I already know she won't. She is the mother of tolerance, the mother of endurance, and even after so many years of not seeing each other, I know it is not a tide I can change.

I cry in response, shake my head, unwilling to accept what she is telling me. She pats my head, a gesture so intimate and nostalgic, I try not to pull away from the generations of cruelty we've endured at each other's hands.

She hushes me. "You don't have to say more. It's been a bitter life for you, just like it's been for me. We're the same."

She tells me her father died and she was married off to my grandfather at sixteen years old. She had no siblings to help her, either. "You can come here every week. Wherever I go, you're welcome. If I move to your big aunt's house, you'll go there, too. Don't worry, mai. You have me now."

In my grandmother's aged face, I see my great-grandmother, my aunts, my uncles, my mother, and I see myself. The self-preservation, the rush of ambition, the worn humanity stare back at me. We are all there, waiting, ready to climb through.

She pats my hand and tells me the story of the banana, the day my mother and I went to my father's family to ask for help. She tells it almost exactly the way my mother told it years ago, full of contempt and anger. She tells it as if she's explaining why my mother is the way she is.

"It was a bitter time, the cruelest your mother had to face alone. Your aunt went and stayed with her for some time, but eventually she had to leave and your mother had to stay there alone, with a child. She couldn't stand it.

"Your hands and feet are exactly like your mother's," she says, wiping tears from my face. She gives my bare foot a shake.

"Do you want something to drink? Tea?" she offers.

We stand and I give her my arm. She leans into me. I take one step and wait for her to follow. The kitchen is less than twenty feet away, but it's a journey to reach. I take another step and she waddles after me. She lowers her voice and says she shares the apartment with a newly immigrated cousin of mine and her husband, who are out working. My cousin works at a nail salon and her husband delivers groceries. They come back only to sleep.

"It's the twins," Nie Nie whispers to me. I lift my head and we listen to the rumbling of small feet across the ceiling. "They scurry back and forth all day long. Always fighting."

Twins run in my family. It's another piece of unexpected information. Upstairs are my cousins, married with children. I wonder if it's the cousin who saved me from drowning in the well. I have so many questions, about them, their parents, my aunts and uncles, my grandfather, my mother, but I hold on to them. They are for another time.

"Here, here." She points to a small tin of tea she can't reach. I unscrew the top and she throws two pinches of loose green leaves into a plastic cup—the red kind that I've used in college for playing beer pong. My mother buys her plasticware so she doesn't have to wash dishes. She tells me to hold it under the lip of the dispenser while she presses a button that dispenses a rush of hot water.

"Careful, careful, hot," she warns tenderly.

Looking around the bare living room, I ask, "What do you do every day? Do—can you read?"

"I never went to school. I have some scriptures memorized." She shuffles over to a plastic drawer in the corner of the room and pulls out a red plastic bag. Inside are thin, worn prayer books inked with tiny Chinese characters. They are so frail they remind me of the fake money used to burn off the debt of past lives, of when I had my fortune told all those years ago.

"What do you do to . . . ?" I press but I don't know how to say "spare time" or "pass the time."

"I pray and I watch TV, when it works." She points to the satellite box, which is unplugged. She tells me about the seniors' community center she goes to every day with Wenzhounese people from back home. It keeps her occupied and active. They take her to the park twice a week.

She shuffles over to a different corner and returns with a walker. She says the American government gave it to her. I understand something then, as she begins to pull out cards from a wallet attached to her phone case. She is being taken care of by Medicare. She repeats that it's all free, along with all the medicine she gets. Everything is covered! I look down at her New York State benefits card, and I see her name written in English for the very first time.

"Ai? What does that mean?"

"You know what that means." She nudges my shoulder. "Ai! Ai!" she shouts.

Love. Her name is Love. I look at her like she's joking, ready to laugh, but she just smiles and tells me it's enough, it's enough. My mother had gotten her passage and a green card. Now the government takes care of her.

One by one, my family had left Wenzhou, and she was the last. But now she is here, with the rest of us. She has her family and kin back. They visit, sit with her, send news and food, and share their lives again. We are no longer in a place she cannot follow or fathom. She sees grandchildren married and watches the next generation of great-grandchildren grow. She had never spoken the desire out loud, but she has caught up with everyone. There is a place for her American dream, too. She chuckles happily and pushes the walker back and forth as if on a runway. She turns to see if I'm watching her. I find myself laughing. Her delight is contagious.

"Now we have it good!" she says, tearing up again.

I blow on the tea leaves until the steam warms my sore eyes. The tea tastes just the way it did in my memories. She leaves her walker and grabs on to my arm to steady herself. We head back to her room, where she begins to tell stories I've been waiting a long time to hear.

Acknowledgments

Writing this book has been easier than living through the experiences on these pages, and that is enormously thanks to my family of writers and friends, who have lifted me with their words, compassion, and unconditional love—the very heart of this story. Thank you: Chris, I have yet to strike the bottom of your patience, your kindness, or your faith; Zino, you took my writing seriously before anyone else did, and I am indebted to your generosity—thank you sister-friend; Amanda, my ride or die bitch, for each and every time you've saved me—from others and from myself.

To Kendra Rajchel, Sara Thomason, N. Michelle AuBuchon, for your sisterhood. To Melissa Febos, Jonathan Vatner, Melissa Faliveno, for your wisdom and guiding light. To Bettina Harriman, Lauren Wallach, Samantha K Smith, Lee Barbour, Kathy Curto, Nicole Dennis-Benn, Mira Ptacin, Dennis Norris II, Amy

Jo Burns for believing what I had to say was worth saying. Thank you for listening, for seeing, and for being my community when I needed it the most, which happens to be all the time.

To every Asian American artist that came before me.

Some of the best years of my life have been at Sarah Lawrence College, in workshop with Vijay Seshadri, JoAnn Beard, Suzanne Gardinier, Nick Flynn, and Stephen O'Connor. I will do my best to teach my students the things you've taught me. To Binghamton University, where I first tasted freedom, and where I belonged.

A thousand thanks to the early believers: Jess Lum, Rose Lee, Cat Li, Lakshmi Panagiotakopoulos, Nina Capacchione, and Gemma Peckham. Our texts, drinks, walks, dinners, trips kept me afloat. In your company, I made a dream come true.

To Jon Antone, for your perspective and friendship. To Bonnie, who keeps me honest and moving forward. To the Clarke-Rajchel family, for treating me like one of your own.

To Laura Pegram at *Kweli Journal*, for your mentorship and enormous heart. To Julia Fierro at Sackett Street Writers' Workshop, for giving me the opportunity to learn and teach. I have worked many jobs, but none has left the same impact as YouVisit—a big shoutout to the YouVisit Fam. You know who you are.

To my family, who I hope will understand why I needed to write this book one day. To my mother, whom I love always. To my stepfather, the only father I've known. To my half siblings, for our shared childhood. And to Mary, wherever you are.

There is no one like the brilliant Duvall Osteen. You are my dream agent. To my editor, Megha Majumdar, for challenging